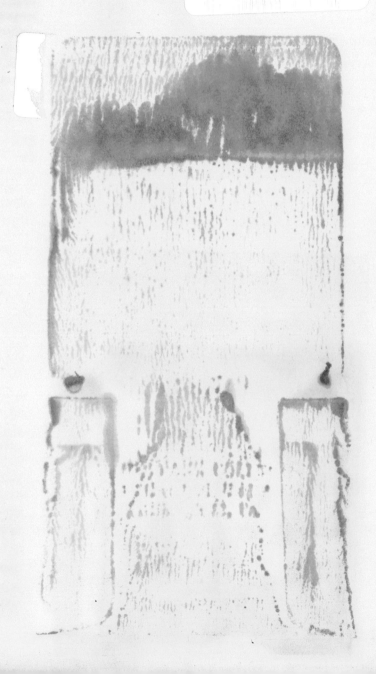

JOSEPH SHUMAN
JOURNALISM COLLECTION

POINT PARK COLLEGE

BOOKS BY

H. L. MENCKEN

These are BORZOI BOOKS *published by* ALFRED A. KNOPF
in New York

H·L·MENCKEN ON MUSIC

PLATE I · H. L. Mencken, *at home on Hollins Street, Baltimore, 1928*

H·L·Mencken
ON MUSIC

A Selection of

HIS WRITINGS ON MUSIC

together with an Account of

H·L·MENCKEN'S MUSICAL LIFE

and a History of

THE SATURDAY NIGHT CLUB

BY

Louis Cheslock

19 61

ALFRED·A·KNOPF NEW YORK

L. C. catalog card number: 61–13949

THIS IS A BORZOI BOOK,

PUBLISHED BY ALFRED A. KNOPF, INC.

FIRST EDITION

HENRY LOUIS MENCKEN

BALTIMORE

September 12, 1880 – January 29, 1956

"A—440" [1]

From a letter by H. L. Mencken to Fanny Butcher, literary critic, Chicago *Tribune*, February 20, 1921.

"I'D RATHER HAVE WRITTEN *any symphony of Brahms' than any play of Ibsen's. I'd rather have written the first movement of Beethoven's Eroica than the Song of Solomon; it is not only far more beautiful, it is also far more profound. A better man wrote it. I believe that Anatole France and Joseph Conrad are the best writers now living, but neither has written anything so good as the first act of "Der Rosenkavalier" or the last ten minutes of "Electra." In music a man can let himself go. In words he always remains a bit stiff and unconvincing."*

[1] "A—440" is standard pitch that sets the tone.

ACKNOWLEDGMENTS

To HENRY MENCKEN'S BROTHER, August, I am profoundly grateful for his abiding interest in this book, and for the innumerable ways in which he helped in its preparation. Also for the many things of which I was unaware he gave freely of his intimate knowledge and experience. To Richard Hart, head of the Literature Department of the Enoch Pratt Free Library, Baltimore, my cordial thanks for making reference works and the Mencken Room available to me often for research. I am sincerely appreciative for permission to use copyrighted material from the publications of Alfred A. Knopf, Inc., N.Y. (the six series of *Prejudices, Happy Days, A Book of Calumny, A Book of Burlesques* and *A Mencken Chrestomathy*, all by H. L. Mencken). Best thanks to the Sunpapers, Baltimore, for permission to reprint numerous articles, as listed; also to the Chicago

Tribune, for two articles, as listed. To Simon and Schuster, Inc., N.Y., my thanks for permission to quote from *Men and Music,* by Wallace Brockway and Herbert Weinstock; also to the *Etude,* magazine, Theodore Presser Co., publisher, to quote as noted. To the Mercantile Safe Deposit and Trust Co., Baltimore, trustee of the Henry L. Mencken estate, sincere appreciation for permission to quote from letters and copyrighted published material. Above all, especial thanks to Henry Mencken, himself, for having committed to print his thoughts on music—the art in which we shared together so many happy hours.

Louis Cheslock

CONTENTS

ILLUSTRATIONS

PRELUDE

PRELUDE

❧

LOUIS CHESLOCK

Music is said to have been Henry Mencken's hobby. This
is true. But it is true only in the sense that he never played
music professionally. For music was to him something more
than a mere hobby.

Even as a youngster he was possessed of a number of
strong creative urges which found their outlets in poetry,
story and play writing, experiments in chemistry, drawing,
and water-color painting. But music was not only his first
true love, it was, indeed, the wellspring of his life—though
not of his livelihood.

The closest he ever came to performing professionally was
sometime in 1933. He was invited by the owner of the Rex
Theater, a movie house in Baltimore, then opening, to appear as solo pianist during the intermission of the premiere
—and at a good fee! Of course, he turned it down. In connection with printed music, his name appears twice as
author of the lyrics of popular songs: "That's His Business"
(1900), music by Julian K. Schaefer, and "The End of it
All" (1904), music by Joseph H. Callahan. Also, Franz
Bornschein made settings for male chorus of two poems

from *Ventures into Verse*, by Mencken: "Arabesque" (1919) and "Ships in Harbor" (1923). But it would be impossible to tabulate the span of time he spent in utmost delight at the piano keyboard, or to reckon the reams of music sheets he filled with his tonal aspirations.

Music is my profession. In my lifelong occupation as composer, performer, and teacher, I have been in close association with countless musical personalities, ranging from beginning students, through enlightened amateurs, to world-renowned practitioners. It is my belief that no one I ever knew loved music more than Mencken. How very deep-rooted was his feeling for the tonal art is best expressed by himself. From his book, *Happy Days* (New York: Alfred A. Knopf; 1940), I select the following few sentences: "My lack of sound musical instruction was really the great deprivation of my life. When I think of anything properly describable as a beautiful idea, it is always in the form of music. I have written and printed probably 10,000,000 words in English, and continue to this day to pour out more and more. But all the same I shall die an inarticulate man, for my best ideas beset me in a language I know only vaguely and speak only like a child."

Music dominated his thinking. A vast number of his nonmusical articles bear titles, expressions, references, and comparisons using music terminology.[2] The highest compli-

---

[2] A few examples: "A Symphony" (actually an ode to Maryland victuals complete with Introduction, Allegro, Larghetto, and Finale!), "Discords in the Harmony" (a comparison of Theodore Roosevelt and William Jennings Bryan), "Decay of a Violin" (decline of Uncle Joe Cannon).

ment he could pay any author was to collate his writing with music. "Reading Cabell, one gets a sense of a flow of harmonious sound. The inner ear responds to a movement that is subtly correct and satisfying. . . . In Cabell there is vastly more than juicy three-four time." A comment on Joseph Conrad's style: "But even speculation could be borne if it ended in discovery—if the final chord was the comforting tonic of C major. But it never is. Nine times out of ten it is a discord without resolution." Of Shakespeare: "A sound sonnet is almost as pleasing an object as a well-written fugue. . . . His music was magnificent, he played superbly upon all the common emotions—and he did it magnificently, he did it with an air."

He had said: "The world presents itself to me, not chiefly as a complex of visual sensations, but as a complex of aural sensations." The sound of tones was to him a lifetime tonic; a soft voice was an almost inexpressible joy. I recall his particular rapture in the singular sound of children practicing piano.

A search through the Mencken ancestry, tracing the line back for more than four hundred years, reveals no evidence or record of a musician in the family. One finds rich merchants, distinguished professors, Doctors of Law, Rectors of Leipzig University, an Archpresbyter of the Cathedral of Marienwerder, notable authors and erudite editors; a member of the Royal Society, a Privy Councilor to August the Strong, a Private Secretary to Frederick the Great, a member of the nobility. However, music having been for centuries a strong factor in the German culture, it can readily be conjectured that it played a role in the lives of most, if not all. Dr. Otto Mencke [3] (1644–1707) was probably the first of the line to change his occupation from commerce to that of learning. He founded and edited the first journal of learning in Germany, *Acta Eruditorum*. He was a professor and later also became Rector at the University of Leipzig.

Lüder Mencke (1658–1726), cousin of Dr. Otto Mencke, was Royal Councilor, and he, too, became Rector of Leipzig University. He was made head of the municipal council committee of the ancient Thomasschule, and it was he who engaged Johann Sebastian Bach in 1723 to supply music to its school and several churches. Bach spent the final 27 years of his life as teacher, organist, composer, choir director and orchestra conductor in its principal church, the Thomaskirche. Here the Leipzig Menckens worshipped, and here also, in this church, is a beautiful Mencken Memorial window, exactly under Old Bach's choir loft!

Anastasius Menckenius (1752–1801) was Private Secretary to Frederick the Great, where, incidentally, Bach's son Karl Philipp Emanuel was, from 1740 to 1767, a court musician and accompanist to Frederick's flute playing. Anastasius married a wealthy widow in 1785, and to the couple was born a son and a daughter. The daughter, inheriting her mother's beauty and fortune, became the darling of Potsdam. Charming Luise Wilhelmine Mencken (1789–1839), married Captain Karl Wilhelm Ferdinand

[3] Mencke is the original spelling of the surname. Later, according to the custom, it was Latinized to Menckenius. When restored to German, the second *n* was retained.

von Bismark, and nine years later became the mother of
Karl Otto Eduard Leopold von Bismark, Germany's famous
"Iron Chancellor."

Henry Mencken's was a wholehearted and infectious
enthusiasm for music, very probably engendered in him in
his early childhood by his father. His father, August, was
an ardent music lover. He had been given some instruction
in violin playing when he was a boy,[4] but gave up when he
discovered he was a "monotone" and possibly "tone-deaf."
The fascination of tones, however, never left him. Occasionally, but in seclusion, he would try fiddling over his *tour de
force*, "Yankee Doodle." But for more reliable musical
rendition he purchased an elaborate Swiss ten-tune music
box—an import in great vogue in those days. It had a name
—*The Sublime Harmonie!* Besides the pin-encrusted
cylinder record, it came equipped with bells, drums, and
zither. Its program consisted of folk songs, mazurkas, polkas,
and waltzes.

At Friederich Knapp's Institute, a private school in Baltimore where Mencken began his education, the day was
always started with singing. Most of the songs were favorite
German folk songs, disciplinarian Herr Knapp leading the
assembled classes playing on his violin, and his beautiful
daughter Bertha accompanying on a parlor organ. In later
life Mencken frequently declared a dislike for singing and
singers, especially the singing of tenors. But actually, and
at the very most, he may have disliked hearing solo singing.

[4] I have one of his instruction books—Mazas' "Violin Method,"
so designated in Henry's handwriting on the flyleaf.

And what his father may have missed in effect upon him with his violin Herr Knapp must surely have fulfilled with his fiddle, for "the sound of horse-hair on catgut" moved him deeply throughout his life.

Very shortly after the turn of the New Year of 1888, Mencken's father had delivered to his home a shining new, black Stieff square piano. Henry, then eight,[5] and his brother Charles, twenty months younger, had their first lessons from a Mr. Maas. The professor was actually the bookkeeper in their father's cigar factory. But knowing something of the mysteries of manipulating the ivory keyboard, he was engaged to give the boys instruction twice a week. For basic technique, Peter's *Eclectic Pianoforte Instructor* and Beyer's *Preliminary School for Piano-Forte* were assigned. Shortly after these, for Henry, there followed Czerny's *School of Velocity*, for which opus he had an especial hatred. Nevertheless, Mr. Maas had his pupils very well along the road to Parnassus in considerably less than a year, at about which time a persistent chest ailment claimed the kindly bookkeeper-musician. Mencken remembered the maestro as an affable and capable man, but even more he recalled his spectacular beard. It was not only extraordinary in size, but it was combed fantastically straight to each side from the middle, in order to cover a pair of slender shoulders.

[5] For more than fifty years Mencken believed that at age six he was an accomplished pianist for a youngster. In delving through some family papers years after his parents had died, he discovered a receipt for the piano dated January 13, 1888, putting his beginning lessons when he was two years older.

Upon the passing of the professor, Mencken's brother Charles stopped taking music lessons, but Henry continued with a new teacher, Miss Lillie Mezger. She was sincerely interested in her charge. The Pratt Library in Baltimore has in its Mencken Room a Christmas gift of a book, *Children's Thoughts in Song and Story*, inscribed by her to *Harry* (as he was spoken of in the family) *Menken!* His first pieces (following the local taste of the time) were such artworks as "Blue Bird Schottische" and "Papa's Waltz"! For what reason Miss Mezger was succeeded by other teachers I do not know; perhaps she married. Following her, however, came a procession of pediculous lady pedagogues. From one of these, in the course of time, Mencken's sister, Gertrude, twenty months younger than her brother Charles, also had some lessons. She did not continue for long. Henry, alone, persevered despite the efforts of his teachers at debasement of both his taste and technique with such ordure as "Black Key Polka," "Monastery Bells," "La Châtelaine," etc.

In those days, as too often, unfortunately, in these days, "taking piano lessons" meant precisely that! Even the most elementary details of what the music was made of was completely ignored by the "lady Leschetizkys." What significance sharps or flats had, which were placed at the head of the staff, was an enigma to the pupil and perhaps also the teacher. Major key—minor key? Major chord—minor chord? Terms—phrase—form, of what concern could these possibly be? Hand position, fingering, and "pieces" were what the tuition was for. Nevertheless, by the time he was ten Henry had gained sufficient skill to be called upon frequently to perform for the guests of his parents. His sight-reading ability and repertoire were growing apace. Although a bit of Beethoven and Mozart had crept into his list of pieces, the treasury, in the main, consisted of mazurkas, polkas, schottisches and waltzes. In time his sphere as performer was enlarged to appearances as pianist at dancing parties in the homes of his friends. Soon his lessons also stopped, but the playing continued. On his own initiative, he persisted in practicing the odious technical exercises.

Although basic theory was still a matter of the future, young Henry, at twelve, had a keen curiosity about it. Also, the urge to compose began to manifest itself. His first piece, neatly written in ink, was a very short "Two-Step" for piano. The next opus, also for piano, but written in pencil, was inscribed at the top, "Tempo di Marchia." [6] Then came a number of waltzes and marches. At the age of fifteen, while a student at the Baltimore Polytechnic Institute, he composed the score for a musical comedy which was produced in the school, and for which he was also librettist and acted as pianist in the orchestra pit. All of these creations, naturally, were the products of trial and error at the keyboard.

On January 13, 1899, Mencken's father died, at the age of forty-five. His namesake and youngest of the four children was then not yet ten. It was the father's influence

---

[6] These and others of his early efforts are in the Mencken Room at the Enoch Pratt Free Library, Baltimore. The calligraphy on all of them looks very nearly professional.

which generated in the children the love of music, and now it was gone. Young August never had music instruction.

Very shortly after his father's death Mencken became a cub reporter for a Baltimore newspaper, the *Herald*. Being a reporter in those days meant working twelve hours a day, minimum, six days a week. Any unfinished work had to be cleared on the so-called "free day." His progress on the paper was astonishingly rapid. There was precious little time left to indulge in composing or for study of the tone art. However, as he got to know the members of the staff more intimately, he discovered to his great delight that a number of them had more than a casual interest in music. The assistant sporting editor, Emanuel Daniel, played the violin. He was variously known as "Schmool," "Schmool Daniel," and "Manuel Daniel." Night editor Isador Goodman played the flute. He had formerly played flute professionally in a circus band. His girl was a singer. It was not long before there were evening meetings to concert their musical efforts. The flute tootling turned out to be poor, the poor girl's singing even worse, so Mencken drowned them out with his stentorian touch. Amiable reporter Lew Schaefer was also a composer of sorts. He had a flair for writing piano pieces for children and revealed each new inspiration to his friend, Henry Mencken.

At the close of 1900, thirty-two-year-old Robert I. Carter came from Cincinnati to become the new managing editor of the *Herald*. Extremely able in his profession and deeply interested and thoroughly seasoned in all the fine arts— most especially in music and the drama—young reporter

Mencken was soon strongly attracted to him. From him he first heard about the fine points in the music of Schubert and Schumann. It was he who first told him about Ibsen and Shaw. From him he learned considerably about the subtleties in craftsmanship of writing and absorbed much of his discriminating taste. Here, indeed, was a gold mine of culture. For his part, Carter at once sensed the immense talents of his protégé and gave him every possible incentive and encouragement. In 1901 he appointed Mencken Sunday Editor of the *Herald*. At the end of 1902 Carter left Baltimore to become managing editor of the New York *Herald*. But the impact of his guidance and influence on Henry Mencken during his brief two-year stay was incalculable.

Also on the *Herald* staff was the Englishman, Owst, as music critic. Wilberfoss G. Owst was a product of typical European rigid and routine drill of those days. He was a well of music theory and "an abyss of thorough-bass." From him Mencken had some help in harmony—and heard much abuse of the music of Brahms.[7] But Irishman Joseph Callahan, Mencken's assistant, whose violation of the violin was almost matchless, was nevertheless a genuine lover of music. Besides, he knew a number of the city's professional and better amateur musicians. It was he who introduced Mencken to many who were to become his lifelong friends through music. The music making and music discussions of his new friends proved to be enchanting and enlightening.

Owst had little taste for the lesser and countless concerts

[7] See page 209 in the Postlude.

then going on in the city. Most of these were organ recitals in remote churches, vocal and instrumental recitals in clubs and lodges, choral and orchestral concerts in the many German music societies, and concerts by Italian bands, which abounded in Baltimore. The repertoires were far from varied, and far also from first quality. Mencken was "borrowed" from the daily city editor and assigned to review or report them. The new head of the *Herald* thought well of his work in this field and, by way of recognition, added a theater roll to his list of duties covering plays, operas, and operettas.

There was no extra pay for the junior critic's services, nor any time allowances made from his regular reporting or editing jobs for the extra evening hours of employment. The concerts and plays were compensation enough. To supplement his meager income of the period, he found time somehow to do an amazing amount of pot-boiler work —brochures for a local piano manufacturer, tracts for one of the town's doctors, pamphlets for a large department store, prefaces to books, and what not!

Mencken managed to get in a few more piano lessons, but his real knowledge of music came mainly from reading. From this time on he accumulated books on orchestration, counterpoint, harmony and history of music, and pocket scores of orchestral works. The materials which he gathered then and during the rest of his life are of the very highest quality. This I know at first hand, as he generously left all his music, music books, and recordings to me. In this fine and comprehensive collection are the most representative works of the foremost musical scholars and composers of the era.

Here, then, was Mencken shortly after the turn of the century, in his early twenties. Despite his heavy hours at work in journalism, his inherent love of music kept his interest bubbling over. In whatever spare time he had he kept studying the music, playing the music, discussing the music, writing on music, and, indeed, composing and arranging music during the incidental periods of the short-lived day. From his own *Ventures Into Verse* he made a partially completed vocal setting of one of his poems, a "Madrigal." For William Watson's poem, "April," he not only completed a voice and piano setting, but made several versions. There are numerous other solo pieces, also some trios for violin, 'cello, and piano. His musical "compositions," naturally, must be regarded as the strivings of his sporadic schooling, and set against the musical background of the town of that time.

In 1904 the city of Baltimore suffered a catastrophic fire, destroying eighty-six blocks in the heart of the city. Among the casualties was the *Herald*, and with it many of Mencken's earliest efforts in journalism. Publication of the paper continued for a while in a temporary relocation, but the struggle for survival was futile, and finally, on June 18, 1906, it collapsed. Mencken had little difficulty in quickly obtaining a new job. He was sought by the editors of the three remaining local papers. For a few weeks he went with the *Evening News* but quit it to go to the Sunpapers. Five years later he was given a column of his own, begun

on May 8, 1911, as the "World in Review." The next day
he changed its name to the "Free Lance." Into this column,
for more than four years, he poured a tremendous variety
of his concepts; and it gained for him a widespread fame.
In addition, he wrote extended Monday Editorials for the
Evening Sun, as well as numerous special articles. He wrote
also for the Chicago *Tribune*, the New York *Evening Mail*,
the New York *American*, and a number of other newspapers. In the ensuing years, book after book of his began
to appear along with his editorship of the *Smart Set* and
American Mercury magazines. Because of the extremely
wide range of his writings, especially in the magazines, he
used a great number of pseudonyms—in fact, a total of
twenty-eight! But only rarely did he use one of them when
writing articles about music: for brief reviews of phonograph records, etc., he sometimes used the pen name of
Atwood C. Bellamy.

Henry Mencken regarded his profession as "critic of
ideas." His thoughts are widely known on a great variety
of subjects: literature, politics, language, religion, medicine,
etc. Generally less known are his articles on music. Some of
these, although half a century old and more, retain a remarkable freshness and pertinence, and contain lucid accounts of
the state of music in Baltimore (ergo, the U.S.) at the turn
of the century. His writing had at all times a uniqueness of
expression and exceptional penetration, besides being enter-
taining and informative.

The following articles appear as Mencken wrote them,
and are headed with the sources from which they are se-

lected. Some he himself condensed and a very few I did also, in order to avoid some repetition. Taking note of the dates on them, one can perceive his progress from venturesome young reporter to erudite critic, whose sound observations and practical ideas still hold good, in many instances, to this day. One should be careful to distinguish between his spoofing and his seriousness; but even in his humor there is a remarkable residue of sage and valuable criticism. I have kept comment on the articles (in footnotes) to a minimum, and only for the purpose of relating some point to the present or setting straight some oversight. These footnotes and the sections without source headings (Prelude, Interludes, and Postlude) are by me.

Baltimore, Maryland 1960

H·L·MENCKEN ON MUSIC

THE THREE B'S

❧

Bach

(1685–1750)

BACH AT BETHLEHEM [1]

From the Baltimore *Evening Sun*, May 30, 1923.
Included in A MENCKEN CHRESTOMATHY, 1949, pp. 543–4.

A DUSTY, bottle-green hillside rising from a river front made harsh and hideous by long lines of blast furnaces; the sunshine blazing down through a haze shot through with wisps of golden orange smoke. Thick woods all the way to the top. In the midst of the solid leafage, rather less than half way up, half a dozen stretches of dingy granite, like outcroppings of the natural rock. Coming closer, one discovers that they are long, bare, stone buildings—laboratories, dor-

---

[1] Mencken attended many of the Bach Festivals at Bethlehem, Pennsylvania, during the great days of Director Dr. Wolle. He went always with a friend—at first with Joseph Hergesheimer, and later often with Alfred A. Knopf. After what was probably his first visit there, in the spring of 1923, he wrote to Knopf: "The Bach jaunt turned out to be very pleasant. We found excellent beer on draught at ten cents a glass. The choruses were superb, but the solo voices singed my kidneys."

mitories, and so on of Lehigh University. Low down the hillside one of them stands up more boldly than the rest. It is Parker Memorial Church, a huge tabernacle in austere, apologetic pseudo-Gothic, with a high square tower—the chapel, in brief, of the university, made wide and deep to hold the whole student body at once, and so save the rev. chaplain the labor of preaching twice.

It is here that the Bach Choir, for years past has been lifting its hosannas to old Johann Sebastian—a curious scene, in more ways than one, for so solemn and ecstatic a ceremonial. Bethlehem, in the main, surely does not suggest the art of the fugue, nor, indeed, any form of art at all. It is a town founded mainly on steel, and it looks appropriately hard and brisk—a town, one guesses instantly, in which Rotarians are not without honor, and the New York Times is read far more than Anatole France. But, as the judicious have observed in all ages, it is hazardous to judge by surfaces. Long before the first steel mill rose by the river, the country all about was peopled by simple Moravians with a zest for praising God by measure, and far back in 1742 they set up a *Singakademie* and began practising German psalm-tunes on Saturday nights. The great-great-grandchild of that *Singakademie* is the Bethlehem Bach Choir of today.

What, indeed, is most astonishing about the whole festival is not that it is given in a Pennsylvania steel town, with the snorting of switching-engines breaking in upon Bach's colossal "Gloria," but that it is still, after all these years, so thoroughly peasant-like and Moravian, so full of home-liness and rusticity. In all my life I have never attended a public show of any sort, in any country, of a more complete and charming simplicity. With strangers crowding into the little city from all directions, and two takers for every seat, and long columns of gabble in the newspapers, the temptation to throw some hocus-pocus about it, to give it a certain florid gaudiness, to bedeck it with bombast and highfalutin must be very trying, even to Moravians. But I can only say that they resist the temptation utterly and absolutely. There is no affectation about it whatever, not even the affectation of solemn religious purpose. Bach is sung in that smoky valley because the people like to sing him, and for no other reason at all. The singers are businessmen and their stenographers, schoolmasters and housewives, men who work in the steel mills and girls waiting to be married. If not a soul came in from outside to hear the music, they would keep on making it just the same, and if the Parker Memorial Church began to disturb them with echoes from empty benches they would go back to their bare Moravian church.

I can imagine no great public ceremonial with less fuss to it. No committee swathed in badges buzzes about; there is none of the usual sweating, fuming and chasing of tails. If one has a ticket, one simply goes to one's pew, plainly numbered on a simple plan, and sits down. If one lacks a ticket, one is quite free to lie in the grass outside, and listen to the music through the open doors. No bawling of hawkers is heard; a single small stand suffices for the sale of programs and scores; there is no effort to rook the stranger.

The cops have nothing to do save tangle the light traffic; there is no confusion, no parade, no noise save from the railroad yards. The conductor slips into his place un-noticed; when a session is over he slips out the same way. It is indeed not a public performance at all, in the custom-ary sense; it is simply the last of this year's rehearsals—and as soon as it is over next year's begin.

BACH AT BETHLEHEM

Extracted from the Baltimore *Evening Sun*, May 21, 1928.

. . . THE MEMBERS of the Bach Choir know the B minor Mass so well that their mere singing of the notes is com-pletely perfect. They never make a ragged entrance and they never waver in tempo. Director John Frederick Wolle is so adept at his drillmaster's job that by the time he steps into his pulpit he is scarcely needed any longer. Unless my eyes and ears gravely deceived me a week ago, I once detected him waving his arms—he uses no baton—off the beat. But the choir kept on singing in perfect time. It would keep on singing in perfect time if the steel mills across the river blew up, and the steeple of the festival church began to wobble. Its *pianissimos* are worth going miles to hear, and when it cuts loose in a *forte* the very firmament trembles.

The accompanying orchestra always suffers greatly by comparison. There is no orchestra of any size in Bethlehem, and so union men have to be brought in from Philadelphia or New York. This year they came from the New York Symphony. In the main, they did well enough, but some of the sounds that came from their first trumpet were extremely disquieting. For a while, indeed, I labored under the delusion that a stupendous B flat clarinet had been introduced into the orchestra, and that it was being played by steam. But such unhappiness had better be forgotten. The Bach scores are immensely difficult, and playing them without adequate rehearsals is surely no enviable job. . . .

BACH AT BETHLEHEM

Extracted from the Baltimore *Evening Sun*, May 20, 1929.

. . . The singing of Johann Sebastian Bach's music at Bethlehem, Pa., goes back to 1742, when the Moravians who had settled there held their first *Singstunde*, but in its present form the Bach Choir is but thirty years old. . . . Its perfections, indeed, are seldom matched, even by much better choirs. Its attack shows an almost mathematical precision, and its divagations from pitch are so rare and inconsiderable as to be unnoticeable. When it tackles a *diminuendo* the fall in sound is beautifully clear and smooth, and when it has a chance to roar it makes the whole Lehigh Valley ring. In all its singing there is tremendous gusto. The occasional hired soloists, mainly bad, suffer vastly by contrast. They do their best but it is usually no more than the best of honest union workmen. The choristers plainly sing because they enjoy it. . . . The choir has sung the B minor Mass 21 times since 1900. It is the annual *pièce de résistance* and occupies both sessions of the second day. Naturally enough, it is sung much better than the things which occupy the first day—usually either the John or Matthew Passions or a series of cantatas. This year the Matthew Passion was done—not badly, to be sure, but still without any distinction. A hired tenor struggled bravely with the long recitatives, but they are essentially unsingable, and so his efforts were more painful than exhilarating. The words of Jesus were sung by the basses in unison—a series of low rumbles, seldom rising to music. The best singing was in the chorales.

In the mass all the solo parts are sung by the appropriate sections of the choir, and so the effect is far better. This year I heard the mass for the third time at Bethlehem, and it seemed to me to be done almost perfectly. The Gloria and the Sanctus were almost overwhelming: it is impossible to imagine anyone with ears sitting unmoved before such stupendous music, so superbly sung. There was magnificent singing, too, in the extraordinarily difficult Et In Unum Dominum, for the two women's choirs alone. This duet makes heavy demands upon singers, orchestra and conductor. All three helped to make it perfect and glorious. . . .

TWO DAYS OF BACH

Extracted from the Baltimore *Evening Sun*, May 25, 1931.

. . . This year's performance, in some ways, was better than usual, and in other ways it was worse. The chorus, it seemed to me, showed a certain weakness, especially in the tenor and alto sections. I suppose the tenor voice is not natural to Pennsylvania Germans; at all events, they do much better as basses. As for the altos, they suffer by the fact that, in general, they seem to be somewhat older than the sopranos; thus the singing of the latter shows more freshness, always an important element in female warbling. But all hands whatever their natural defects, yet sing with complete enthusiasm and remarkable skill. The attack of the choir is as sharp as a sword-stroke; it responds to its leader perfectly; it never wanders from the key.

There have been times in the past when the B minor Mass was badly damaged by a bad orchestral accompaniment, but this year the boys of the union—all of them, I believe, from the Philadelphia Orchestra—played superbly. Such lovely tones as came from the oboe, the first flute, the horns and the trumpets are seldom heard in this world. Nor must I forget the excellent piano accompaniment of Miss Pauline Detterer in the cantatas, or the good work of the two brethren who played bull-fiddles—a most important matter in doing Bach.

Of the soloists the only one who achieved any genuine glory was the bass, Charles Trowbridge Tittmann, of Washington. He is now an old hand at Bethlehem, and sings the fiendishly difficult music of the cantatas with ease and authority. He has a big voice, and is not overwhelmed, as his tenor colleagues almost always are, by contrast with the great blast of the chorus. Unluckily, the English words used in the cantatas are completely idiotic, and Mr. Tittmann often had to sing such stuff as this:

> *Sergeant! Hell-horror!*
> *Dost not feel terror?*

The music to this drivel is magnificent, but the words will not down. As for me, I'd much prefer to hear Dr. Tittmann sing "Im Tiefen Keller." The lady soloists have even worse to sing. In the cantata called "Wir müssen durch viel Trübsal" the contralto must struggle with this:

> *I'd fain earthward instant fly.*
> *Idle Mammon, hence from me!*

Alas, the German original is almost as bad! In the same cantata the soprano gets a far better break. The words she has to sing are almost intelligent, and the accompaniment by flute and oboe is unutterably charming. This aria was sung by Mrs. Ernestine Hohl Eberhard, a member of the choir.

On the first day of the two-day festival Dr. Wolle put on nine cantatas—a somewhat heavy dose. Bach wrote 200 altogether, and every one of them, in some way or other, is beautiful, but they tend to seem monotonous when strung in a chain, and the difficulties of the music, especially to the soloists, are accentuated. Some of the arias are really almost unsingable; even a piccolo player, tackling them, would get out of breath. The chorales go better. Dr. Wolle prints the tunes in his programme, has the audience rise when they are sung, and evidently expects it to join in. This year it stood mute, though most of the tunes are quite simple. But it always leaped up with alacrity, plainly glad to get off the hard church benches for a few minutes. . . .

(Interlude)

IT IS RECOGNIZED, historically, that the epitome of court-
liness and charm in music was reached in the symphonic works of Mozart and Haydn. It is true, to a
certain extent, that Beethoven's first two symphonies
link onto the music of these masters. But with the
birth of the *Eroica* there came a cleavage of colossal
force and abruptness. Music was forever turned to its
new course. At long last it was taken away from the
effete few—mainly royalty—and given to all mankind.
Immediately, within the opening few measures of the
Eroica, one is aware of being in the presence of a deep-
feeling, humane, and powerful personality. No longer
now the formalized, "correct" harmonic progressions,
but instead, dramatic successions to stormy and ex-
plosive impacts of daringly dissonant climaxes. Consider the boldness of this Beethoven work. Every con-
stituent element in the complex of music is pushed
and driven to further frontiers. At the summit of the
climax of the first movement, and in full force,
Beethoven sounds an inverted, shrieking seventh chord
of F-A-C-E, and tops it off in the flutes with the dissonant E and F wedded to each other! At the junction
of the development and recapitulation, even though
marked *pianissimo,* the tonic chord of E flat clashes
against its dominant seventh. Contemplate the rugged-
ness of the rhythms, and the vividness of the dynamics.
The unexpected and dazzling modulations actually

shocked the venturesome Viennese of the first audience. It was considered to be a composition which
"lost itself in lawlessness"! Nevertheless, they felt compelled to remain and listen to this completely uncon-
ventional music, despite their resentment, because it
was certainly evident to them that Beethoven had
something of vast importance to say, and was saying
it! But the reaction did not die down soon. It lasted
for more than half a century. How full of error are
these sample comments of the times:

From a letter by a Viennese to the Leipzig paper,
Allegemeine Musicalische Zeitung, February 13, 1805,
following a private concert in the home of Prince
Lobkowitz: "The writer belongs to Beethoven's warm-
est admirers, but in the present work (Eroica symphony) he finds very much that is odd and harsh,
enormously increasing in difficulty of comprehension
of the music, and obscuring its unity almost entirely."
The critic of the Vienna paper, *Freymüthige*, following the first public performance of the work on Sunday,
April 7, 1805, in the Theatre-an-der-Wien, said, among
other things: "The connection is often disrupted entirely, and the inordinate length of this longest,[2] and
perhaps most difficult of all symphonies, wearies even
the *cognoscenti*, and is unendurable to the mere music-
lover. It fears that if Beethoven continues on his pres-

---

[2] To the many complaints that his symphony was of too great
length, Beethoven retorted: "If I write a symphony an hour long
it will be found short enough!"

ent path both he and the public will be the sufferers.
The public and Herr van Beethoven, who conducted,
were not satisfied with each other this evening: the
public thought the symphony too heavy, too long, and
Beethoven himself, too discourteous, because he did
not nod his head in recognition of the applause which
came from a portion of the audience."

At the first rehearsal of the symphony, Ferdinand
Ries, good friend and pupil of Beethoven, recalls: "In
the first Allegro occurs a wicked whim of Beethoven's
for the horn; in the second part, several measures before
the theme recurs in its entirety, Beethoven has the
horn suggest it at a place where the violins are still
holding a second chord. To one unfamiliar with the
score this must always sound as if the horn player had
made a miscount and entered at the wrong place. At
the rehearsal, which was horrible, but at which the horn
player made this entry correctly, I stood beside Beethoven and, thinking that a blunder had been made, I
said: "Can't the damned hornist count?—it sounds
infamously false!" I think I came pretty close to re-
ceiving a box on the ear. Beethoven did not forgive
the slip for a long time."

Part of the first public audience felt that, "by means
of strange modulations and violent transitions, by com-
bining the most heterogeneous elements, as for instance
when a pastoral in the largest style is ripped up by the
basses, by three horns, etc., a certain undesirable originality may be achieved without much trouble."

Schindler, Beethoven's companion and copyist, says that it (the *Eroica*) was held in horror by Beethoven's old enemy, Dionys Weber, head of the Conservatorium at Prague, considering it a "dangerously immoral composition!"

Mencken's taste in music was universal in the fullest sense. His predilection for the so-called "classics" was natural and wholehearted. According to the mood or occasion, however, he could appreciate with the same genuineness Jerome Kern's "Old Man River," a Strauss waltz, or a Rossini overture, as any extended opus of the acknowledged "Masters." But of all the music he knew —and he knew amazingly much—the one work he most revered was Beethoven's *Eroica* symphony and, in particular, the first movement.

In an article in the music magazine *Etude* of January, 1931, he was asked: "If you were assured by your physician that you had only twenty-four more hours to live and you were given the opportunity to hear just one piece of music, what would you select?" His reply, in part, was: "Your question is somewhat difficult. My first choice is the first movement of the "Eroica" symphony, played by any good orchestra." At the same time he admitted leaning heavily to Schubert's quintette with the two 'cellos, as well as to other music by Schubert; but felt "it would be a dreadful business to make that choice in actuality." Undoubtedly this was the most guarded statement of his preference I have ever encountered. Unfailingly, in all his other expressions, there was only complete and unbounded enthusiasm for Beethoven, the man and his music—and notably this opening movement of the third symphony. Time and time again he stated, in the printed and pronounced word, that this one piece was to him the pinnacle of musical achievement. To appreciate the full extent of his profound admiration for this opus one must have *heard* him express himself upon it. The apex of his ecstasy was reserved for this work, and his voice was imbued with a warmth that made his singing of the themes tingle with an inspired and almost instrumental expressiveness. More—as he sang the music the burst and bounce on the *sforzati* at the top of each climbing chord was a marvel to hear and behold. The gesturing alone compared favorably with the best of any of our present-day world-renowned calisthenic orchestral conductors! And never in his performance at the piano was the dynamic level irresolute, as by nature and by habit he was not one to "soft-pedal" anything![3]

What was it then, and why was it that Beethoven— and in particular this piece—fired in him such rapture? My guess is that there is here a parallel affinity of personality and purpose. Both Beethoven and Mencken were possessed with strong feelings of revolt against the old order which existed in their respective creative

---

[3] How Mencken became "a slave to the forte pedal"—see "The Ruin of an Artist," in his book, *Happy Days* (New York: Alfred A. Knopf; 1940, p. 193).

fields. In the early era of each, only clichés and stock sentiment succeeded and prevailed. Change was long overdue in each instance. The time was ripe to turn to new paths, and for the appearance of new pathfinders. These leaders, besides being original, needed to be hardy and without fear. And this, each in his own way, was.

In the same sense that Beethoven was aware of the language of sound, Mencken was aware of the sound of language. In the same way that Beethoven would not and could not conform to the threadbare conventions of his art, neither could Mencken countenance the continuance of Victorianism in any of its forms. Both were disturbers of complacency. They were bold, forthright, and strong personalities. Both gave battle—stormy, vigorous, and even brutal. Neither cared whether what he had to say was liked or not. Each, in his time, obeyed the inevitable compulsion to say what he believed, and what he had been born to say. There was no attempt to plush-cover the hammer-head. If a point had to be driven home, then the steel had to be hard. When each had ended his encounter the old order was forever over, and a new sound was heard in the land!

Beethoven

(1 7 7 0 – 1 8 2 7)

From PREJUDICES: FIFTH SERIES, 1926, pp. 87–94.
First printed in part in the Baltimore *Evening Sun*, April 24, 1922,
and in part in *American Mercury*, April, 1926, pp. 509–10,
also in A MENCKEN CHRESTOMATHY, 1949, pp. 523–7.

BEETHOVEN was one of those lucky men whose stature, viewed in retrospect, grows steadily. How many movements have there been to put him on the shelf? At least a dozen in the hundred years since his death. There was one in New York in 1917, launched by idiot critics and supported by war fever; his place, it appeared, was to be taken by such prophets of the new enlightenment as Stravinsky. The net result of that movement was simply that the best orchestra in America went to pot—and Beethoven survived unscathed. Surely the Nineteenth Century was not deficient in master musicians. It produced Schubert, Schumann, Chopin, Wagner and Brahms, to say nothing of a whole horde of Dvořáks, Tschaikowskys, Debussys, Verdis, and Puccinis. Yet it gave us nothing better than the first movement of the Eroica. That movement, the first challenge of the new music, remains its last word. It is the noblest piece of absolute music ever written in sonata form, and it is the noblest piece of programme music. In Beethoven, indeed, the distinction between the two became purely imaginary. Everything he wrote was, in a way, programme music, including even the first two symphonies, and everything was absolute music.

It was a bizarre jest of the gods to pit Beethoven, in his first days in Vienna, against Papa Haydn. Haydn was undeniably a genius of the first water, and, after Mozart's death, had no apparent reason to fear a rival. If he did not actually create the symphony as we know it today, then he at least enriched the form with its first genuine masterpieces —and not with a scant few, but literally with dozens. Tunes of the utmost loveliness gushed from him like oil from a well. More, he knew how to manage them; he was a master of musical architectonics. But when Beethoven stepped in, poor old Papa had to step down. It was like pitting a gazelle against a bull. One colossal bellow, and the combat was over. Musicians are apt to look at it as a mere contest of technicians. They point to the vastly greater skill and ingenuity of Beethoven—his firmer grip upon his materials, his greater daring and resourcefulness, his far better understanding of dynamics, rhythms and clang-tints —in brief, his tremendously superior musicianship. But that was not what made him so much greater than Haydn— for Haydn, too, had his superiorities; for example, his far readier inventiveness, his capacity for making better tunes. What lifted Beethoven above the old master was simply his greater dignity as a man. The feelings that Haydn put into tone were the feelings of a country pastor, a rather civilized stockbroker, a viola player gently mellowed by Kulmbacher. When he wept it was the tears of a woman who has discovered another wrinkle; when he rejoiced it was with the joy of a child on Christmas morning. But the feelings that Beethoven put into his music were the feelings of a god. There was something Olympian in his snarls and rages, and there was a touch of hell-fire in his mirth.

It is almost a literal fact that there is no trace of cheapness in the whole body of his music. He is never sweet and romantic; he never sheds conventional tears; he never strikes orthodox attitudes. In his lightest moods there is the immense and inescapable dignity of ancient prophets. He concerns himself, not with the transient agonies of romantic love, but with the eternal tragedy of man. He is a great tragic poet, and like all great tragic poets, he is obsessed by a sense of the inscrutable meaninglessness of life. From the Eroica onward he seldom departs from that theme. It roars through the first movement of the C minor, and it comes to a stupendous final settlement in the Ninth. All this, in his day, was new in music, and so it caused murmurs of surprise and even indignation. The step from Mozart's Jupiter to the first movement of the Eroica was uncomfortable; the Viennese began to wriggle in their stalls. But there was one among them who didn't wriggle, and that was Franz Schubert. Turn to the first movement of his Unfinished or to the slow movement of his Tragic, and you will see how quickly the example of Beethoven was followed—and with what genius. There was a long hiatus after that, but eventually the day of November 6, 1876, dawned in Karlsruhe, and with it came the first performance of Brahms' C minor. Once more the gods walked in the concert hall. They will walk again when another Brahms is born, and not before. For nothing can come out of an artist that is not in the man. What ails the music of all the Tschaikowskys, Mendelssohns—and Chopins? What ails it is that it is the music of shallow men. It is often, in its way, lovely. It bristles with charming musical ideas. It is infinitely ingenious and workmanlike. But it is hollow, at bottom, as a bull by an archbishop. It is music of second-rate men.

Beethoven disdained all their artifices: he didn't need them. It would be hard to think of a composer, even of the fourth rate, who worked with thematic material of less intrinsic merit. He borrowed tunes wherever he found them; he made them up out of snatches of country jigs; when he lacked one altogether he contented himself with a simple phrase, a few banal notes. All such things he viewed simply as raw materials; his interest was concentrated upon their use. To that use of them he brought the appalling powers of his unrivalled genius. His ingenuity began where that of other men left off. His most complicated structures retained the overwhelming clarity of the Parthenon. And into them he got a kind of feeling that even the Greeks could not match; he was preëminently a modern man, with all trace of the barbarian vanished. Into his gorgeous music there went all of the high skepticism that was of the essence of the Eighteenth Century, but into it there also went a new enthusiasm, the new determination to challenge and beat the gods, that dawned with the Nineteenth.

The older I grow, the more I am convinced that the most portentous phenomenon in the whole history of music was the first public performance of the Eroica on April 7, 1805. The manufacturers of programme notes have swathed that gigantic work in so many layers of banal legend and speculation that its intrinsic merits have been almost forgotten. Was it dedicated to Napoleon I? If so, was the dedication sincere or ironical? Who cares—that is, who with ears? It might have been dedicated, just as well, to Louis XIV, Paracelsus or Pontius Pilate. What makes it worth discussing, today and forever, is the fact that on its very first page Beethoven threw his hat into the ring and laid his claim to immortality. Bang!—and he is off. No compromise! No easy bridge from the past! The second symphony is already miles behind. A new order of music has been born. The very manner of it is full of challenge. There is no sneaking into the foul business by way of a mellifluous and disarming introduction; no preparatory hemming and hawing to cajole the audience and enable the conductor to find his place in the score. Nay! Out of silence comes the angry crash of the tonic triad, and then at once, with no pause, the first statement of the first subject—grim, domineering, harsh, raucous, and yet curiously lovely—with its astounding collision with that electrical C sharp. The carnage has begun early; we are only in the seventh measure. In the thirteenth and fourteenth comes the incomparable roll down the simple scale of E flat—and what follows is all that has ever been said, perhaps all that ever *will* be said, about music-making in the grand manner. What was afterward done, even by Beethoven, was done in the light of that perfect example. Every line of modern music that is honestly music bears some sort of relation to that epoch-making first movement.

The rest of the Eroica is Beethovenish, but not quintessence. There is a legend that the funeral march was put in simply because it was a time of wholesale butchery, and funeral marches were in fashion. No doubt the first-night audience in Vienna, shocked and addled by the piled-up defiances of the first movement, found the lugubrious strains grateful. But the *scherzo?* Another felonious assault upon poor Papa Haydn! Two giants boxing clumsily, to a crazy piping by an orchestra of dwarfs. No wonder some honest Viennese in the gallery yelled: "I'd give another kreutzer if the thing would stop!" Well, it stopped finally, and then came something reassuring—a theme with variations. Everyone in Vienna knew and esteemed Beethoven's themes with variations. He was, in fact, the rising master of themes with variations in the town. But a joker remained in the pack. The variations grew more and more complex and surprising. Strange novelties got into them. The polite exercises became tempestuous, moody, cacophonous, tragic. At the end a harsh, hammering, exigent row of chords— the C minor symphony casting its sinister shadow before.

It must have been a great night in Vienna. But perhaps not for the actual Viennese. They went to hear "a new grand symphony in D sharp" (*sic!*). What they found in the Theatre-an-der-Wien was a revolution.

Old Ludwig and his Ways

Mencken's review of *The Unconscious Beethoven*, by Ernest Newman
(New York: Alfred A. Knopf; 1927).
Appeared in *American Mercury*, June, 1927.

IN MR. NEWMAN's judgment Beethoven's natural tendency to turn his back upon the world was promoted by a physical infirmity—the syphilis that prevented his marriage, and was the cause of his deafness and death. How he became infected we don't know: probably as an incident of some otherwise harmless youthful folly. But the fact of his infection seems to be quite plain, despite the effort of certain sentimental German pathologists to talk it into improbability. Beethoven unquestionably suffered from the malady of kings, messiahs and philosophers, and it was chiefly responsible for his life-long unhappiness and his intense and almost murderous misanthrophy. In particular it made him a misogynist, especially when he had to deal with ladies known to be of excessive amiability. That is why, according to Mr. Newman, he hated the wives of his two brothers, and wasted so much of his time and energy trying to do them injury. He believed that they were loose, and that their looseness was dangerous. Maintaining this thesis, he often permitted his indignation to carry him beyond the letter of the record, but there is every reason to believe that the thesis itself was quite sound.

Beethoven, though certainly not a courtier, was nevertheless a man of honor: no bounder could have written his incomparable music. The average musician of his time, finding himself luetic by God's will, would have swallowed

a few pounds of mercury, and then affianced himself cheerfully to the first woman willing to marry him. But old Ludwig was strangely modern and scientific, beside having a
tender conscience, and so he refrained from connubial
bliss. His course did him honor, but made him very un-
happy. For there was probably never another man in the
world who needed the ministrations of an efficient German
wife as much as he did. He had absolutely no capacity for the
round of petty but invaluable tricks that make up the business of housekeeping. He always forgot to have the windows
washed. He never remembered to change his shirt. He had
the fire roaring on hot days, and let it go out on cold days.
He managed servants by alternately over-paying them and
heaving crockery at them. So he lived like a pig all his days,
in the utmost mental and physical discomfort. His household was so forbidding that his nephew preferred suicide to
living in it. Worse, the poor fellow was always falling in love.
His heart went pitter-pat every time he saw a pretty girl,
which, in Vienna, was very often. Thus he became a
Freudian case, and led a life of almost unmitigated misery.
To that misery we must lay his sterile years, when he could
not write at all, and the lamentable fact that he wrote but
nine symphonies, to Mozart's thirty and Haydn's sixty.[4]
But to it, also, we must lay much of the splendor of what
he actually got upon paper. No healthy and happy man
could have matched it, for the gods are jealous of happiness,
and punish it with dullness. When, in the years to come,
some second Beethoven writes a piece of music as stupen-

---

[4] Actually, Mozart wrote 41 symphonies, and Haydn, 104.

dous as the first movement of the Eroica, it will be found,
on inquiry, that he has lost his girl to a handsomer man,
and the chances are at least even that his Wassermann will
turn out to be positive.

Beethoveniana

Mencken's reviews of *Beethoven the Creator*, by Romain Rolland
(New York: Harper & Brothers; 1929)
and *Beethoven, the Man who Freed Music*, by Robert Haven Schauffler
(Garden City: Doubleday, Doran & Company; 1929).
Appeared in *American Mercury*, December, 1929.

. . . M. ROLLAND, despite the size of his book makes no
effort to cover Beethoven's whole career. He begins with the
Eroica and ends with the "Fidelio" fiasco, surely a small
enough segment. Indeed, he discusses only three works at
any length: the Eroica, the Appassionata, and "Fidelio."
The last-named he puts far higher than any other critic
that I am aware of. He speaks of it as "the king-oak of the
forest", and deplores the fact that Wagner, "encumbered
with metaphysic", could not grasp its "grand and classical
humanity." It is, he says "the monument of a better Europe
of which, on the threshold of the Nineteenth Century,
Goethe and Beethoven had a glimpse, and that a hundred
years of subsequent torment have not been able to realize."
Following it, there appeared a demoniac element in Beethoven's writing, especially in the Rasoumovsky quartettes,
and the "hinges of his soul" began to grate. It may be so, but
I must confess that the evidence is not altogether clear to
me. I am rather inclined to believe, indeed, that there is

quite as much of this demonism in the first movement of the
Eroica, and notably in the coda thereof, as you will find in
all that comes after, not forgetting even the last quartettes.
M. Rolland is all for believing that Beethoven was made
deaf, not by anything so prosaic as microbes or their toxins,
but by the sheer power of his own genius. To support that
notion he resorts to the testimony of East Indian mystics
who say that they "come out of the spells of Yoga with eyes
red and bleeding, as if eaten by ants." Old Ludwig, of
course, knew nothing of such spells, but when he sat down
to compose music "the hammering of the rhythm" and
"the sensuous heat of the orchestral color" worked much
the same effect upon him, and so his brain was heavily
battered, and his auditory centers began to disintegrate. It
is all very lovely, but my duty to my art compels me to add
that, with all due respect for M. Rolland, it strikes me as
hard to distinguish from damned foolishness.

All the critics of Beethoven, alas, seem to be tempted to
such highfalutin stuff. Even Mr. Schauffler shows the
stigma, though he is naturally a sober fellow, and his account of Beethoven's life is marked by a considerable common sense. It is when he essays to analyze the Master's
music that he begins to see things. What he sees chiefly
is a long series of recurring patterns. These he calls, at
different times, germ-motives or source-motives. That Beethoven actually made use of them is of course familiar to
everyone, for a shining example glares at the world from the
first two measures of the C minor symphony. But that he
was at pains to stick them into everything he wrote, some-

times so stealthily that it is hard to unearth them—this seems to me to be somewhat unlikely. The fact is that, like any other composer, he had a natural weakness for certain idioms, and that their appearance in his scores is often evidence, not that he was trying to out-smart all other composers, but simply that he was taking the easiest way. In many cases those idioms were not his own inventions, but came from the common store of music. That Beethoven preferred this one to that one is probably true, and that he used all of them with far greater skill than anyone else is also true, but that he attached any esoteric significance to them is highly improbable. Thus I find it impossible to follow Mr. Schauffler all the way. But his industry is certainly to be praised, and with it his genuine delight in Beethoven. If his work accomplishes no other good, it may at least induce other music-lovers to give hard study to the scores. They well deserve it, for they are full of gorgeous surprises and no man knows them so well completely.

(Interlude)

MENCKEN has often been compared with Shaw. In a number of instances, their courses run parallel. One of these coincidences was that as young journalists both served as music critics for newspapers. The background and equipment each brought to his task were not too dissimilar. But in their appreciation of Brahms they differed very widely, indeed!

Shaw had a real aversion to Brahms, the man as well

as his music. He considered the composer possessed of "a commonplace mind." His music had "nothing better in the way of ideas to express than incoherent commonplace"—"aberrations into pure stupidity"!

A few more of Shaw's pronouncements on Brahms follow (from his week-to-week criticisms in *The World*, London, 1890–93):

"There are some sacrifices which should not be demanded twice from any man; and one of them is listening to Brahms' Requiem. On some future evening, perhaps, when the weather is balmy, and I can be accommodated with a comfortable armchair, an interesting book, and all the evening newspapers, I may venture; but last week I should have required a requiem for myself if I had attempted such a feat of endurance. I am sorry to have to play the "disgruntled" critic over a composition so learnedly contrapuntal, not to say fugacious; but I really cannot stand Brahms as a serious composer." (December 24, 1890)

"Brahms' Requiem has not the true funeral relish: it aims at the technical traditions of requiem composition rather than the sensational, and is so execrably and ponderously dull that the very flattest of funerals would seem like a ballet, or at least a *danse macabre* after it."

(November 9, 1892)

"I wonder what Mr. Statham would think of me if I objected to Brahms' Requiem, not on the ground that

PLATE II · An arrangement by Mencken for violin, 'cello, and piano (around 1902) of Beethoven's Symphony No. I (last movement, measures 26 through 50)

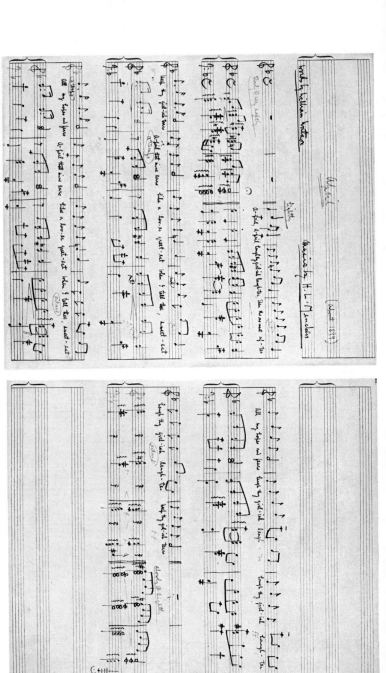

PLATE III · One of several versions of Mencken's setting for voice and piano to William Watson's poem "April"

it bores me to distraction, but as a violation of the laws of nature."

(May 31, 1893)

And now, Mencken on Brahms . . .

Brahms

(1833–97)

From *Five Little Excursions*, PREJUDICES: SIXTH SERIES, 1927, pp. 163–9.
First printed in the Baltimore *Evening Sun*, August 2, 1926.
Included in A MENCKEN CHRESTOMATHY, 1949, pp. 532–5.

MY EXCUSE for writing of the above gentleman is simply that, at the moment, I can think of nothing else. A week or so ago, on a Baltimore Summer evening of furious heat, I heard his sextet for strings, opus 18, and ever since then it has been sliding and pirouetting through my head. I have gone to bed with it and I have got up with it. Not, of course, with the whole sextet, nor even with any principal tune of it, but with the modest and fragile little episode at the end of the first section of the first movement—a lowly thing of nine measures, thrown off like a perfume, so to speak, from the second subject.

What is the magic in such sublime trivialities? Here is a tune so slight and unassuming that it runs to but nine measures and uses but six of the twelve tones in the octave, and yet it rides an elderly and unromantic man, weighing 180 pounds and with a liver far beyond pills or prayer, as if it were the very queen of the succubi. Is it because I have a delicately sensitive ear? Bosh! I am almost tone-deaf. Or a tender and impressionable heart? Bosh again! Or a beautiful soul? *Dreimal* bosh! No theologian not in his cups would insure me against Hell for cent per cent. No, the answer is to be found in the tune, not in the man. Trivial in seeming, there is yet in it the power of a thousand horses. Modest, it speaks with a clarion voice, and having spoken, it is remembered. Brahms made many another like it. There is one at the beginning of the trio for violin, 'cello and piano, opus 8—the loveliest tune, perhaps, in the whole range of music. There is another in the slow movement of the quintet for piano and strings, opus 34. There is yet another in the double concerto for violin and 'cello, opus 102—the first subject of the slow movement. There is one in the coda of the Third Symphony. There is an exquisite one in the Fourth Symphony. But if you know Brahms, you know all of them quite as well as I do. Hearing him is as dangerous as hearing Schubert. One does not go away filled and satisfied, to resume business as usual in the morning. One goes away charged with a something that remains in the blood a long while, like the toxins of love or the pneumococcus. If I had a heavy job of work to do on the morrow, with all hands on deck and the cerebrum thrown into high, I'd certainly not risk hearing any of the Schubert string quartets, or the incomparable quintet with the extra 'cello, or the slow movement of the Tragic Symphony. And I'd hesitate a long time before risking Brahms.

It seems an astounding thing that there was once a war over him, and that certain competent musicians, otherwise sane, argued that he was dull. As well imagine a war over Beauvais Cathedral or the Hundred-and-third Psalm. The contention of these foolish fellows, if I recall it aright, was that Brahms was dull in his development sections— that he flogged his tunes to death. I can think of nothing more magnificently idiotic. Turn to the sextet that I have mentioned, written in the early 60's of the last century, when the composer was barely thirty. The development section of the first movement is not only fluent and workmanlike: it is a downright masterpiece. There is a magnificent battle of moods in it, from the fiercest to the tenderest, and it ends with a coda that is sheer perfection. True enough, Brahms had to learn—and it is in the handling of thematic material, not in its invention, that learning counts. When he wrote his first piano trio, at twenty-five or thereabout, he started off, as I have said, with one of the most entrancing tunes ever put on paper, but when he came to develop it his inexperience threw him, and the result was such that years later he rewrote the whole work.

But by the time he came to his piano concerto in D he was the complete master of his materials, and ever thereafter he showed a quality of workmanship that no other composer has ever surpassed, not even Beethoven. The first movement of the Eroica, I grant you, is *sui generis*: it will never be matched until the time two great geniuses collide again. But what is in the rest of the first eight symphonies, even including the Fifth and Ninth, that is clearly better than what is in the four of Brahms? The first performance of his First, indeed, was as memorable an event in the history of music as the first performance of the Eroica. Both were frantically denounced, and yet both were instantaneous successes. I'd rather have been present at Karlsruhe on November 6, 1876, I think, than at the initiation of General Pershing into the Elks. And I'd rather have been present at Vienna on April 7, 1805, than at the landing of Columbus.

More than any other art, perhaps, music demands brains. It is full of technical complexities. It calls for a capacity to do a dozen things at once. But most of all it is revelatory of what is called character. When a trashy man writes it, it is trashy music. Here is where the immense superiority of such a man as Brahms becomes manifest. There is less trashiness in his music than there is in the music of any other man ever heard of, with the sole exception, perhaps, of Johann Sebastian Bach. It was simply impossible for him, at least after he had learned his trade, to be obvious or banal. He could not write even the baldest tune without getting into it something of his own high dignity and profound seriousness; he could not play with that tune, however light his mood, without putting an austere and noble stateliness into it. Hearing Brahms, one never gets any sense of being entertained by a clever mountebank. One is facing a supe-

rior man, and the fact is evident from the first note. I give
you his "Deutsches Requiem" as an example. There is not
a hint of what is commonly regarded as religious feeling in
it. Brahms, so far as I know, was not a religious man. Nor
is there the slightest sign of the cheap fustian of conventional patriotism. Nevertheless, a superb emotion is there—
nay, an overwhelming emotion. The thing is irresistibly
moving. It is moving because a man of the highest intellectual dignity, a man of exalted feelings, a man of brains,
put into it his love for and pride in his country.[5]

But in music emotion is only half the story. Mendelssohn
had it, and yet he belongs to the second table. Nor is it a
matter of mere beauty—that is, of mere sensuous loveliness.
If it were, then Dvořák would be greater than Beethoven,
whose tunes are seldom inspired, and who not infrequently
does without them altogether. What makes great music
is simply the thing I have mentioned: brains. The greatest
musician is a man whose thoughts and feelings are above
the common level, and whose language matches them.
What he has to say comes out of a wisdom that is not ordinary. Platitude is impossible to him. Above all, he is a master of his craft, as opposed to his art. He gets his effects in
new, difficult and ingenious ways—and they convince one
instantly that they are inevitable. One can easily imagine
improvements in the human eye, and in the Alps, and in
the art of love, and even in the Constitution, but one cannot imagine improvement in the first movement of the

[5] It is a "Deutches" (German) Requiem because the text is in
the German language instead of the traditional Latin.

Eroica. The thing is completely perfect, even at the places where the composer halts to draw breath. Any change in it would damage it. But what is inevitable is never obvious. John Doe would not and could not write thus. The immovable truths that are there—and there are truths in the arts as well as in theology—became truths when Beethoven formulated them. They did not exist before. They cannot perish hereafter.

. . . End of Mencken on Brahms.

MORE

OF THE MASTERS

❦

Schubert

(1 7 9 7 – 1 8 2 8)

From the Baltimore *Evening Sun*, November 19, 1928.

A HUNDRED years ago today, in Vienna, Franz Schubert died. He was one of the greatest geniuses the world has ever seen, but he was a poor man, and so his funeral was very modest. At first his father, who was a schoolmaster, planned to bury him under the floor of a parish church, but someone suggested that a more suitable place would be somewhere near Beethoven, who had died the year before. So a grave was found in the Währing cemetery, and there he was planted, and still rests. His funeral cost 70 florins. When, a week or so later, his estate was listed for the public records, it was found to be 60 florins. Thus he died bankrupt.

But it is not to be assumed from this that Schubert, in life, had been unknown, or neglected. Far from it. His immense talent was recognized when he was a boy of 15, and by the time he was 25 he was already something of a celebrity. The Viennese certainly had ears: they could hear his music, and hearing it was enough to convince anyone that it was good. But Schubert himself was the sort of man who, in all societies and at all times, finds it hard to get along. He was so modest that it was simply impossible for him to push himself; he even shrank from meeting Beethoven, who needed only a glance at his songs to see his genius. Worse, he wrote so much that he constantly broke his own market. There were always stacks of Schubert manuscripts in waiting, and so the publishers paid very little for what they took.

This fecundity ran to almost incredible lengths. In fifteen years Schubert wrote more than 1,200 compositions, some of them full-length symphonies. His songs run to at least 600, and he wrote the astonishing number of 146 in a single year, 1815. In the August of that year he wrote 29, and on one day he wrote 8. It seems unbelievable, but it is a fact. Some of these songs were better than others, but not one of them was downright bad. The best are among the imperishable glories of the human race. They are wholly and overwhelmingly lovely. No one has ever written lovelier.

Schubert was poor, but he had what must have been, at least in its externals, a pleasant life. A bachelor at large in the most charming of cities, with a father and brothers who appreciated him and plenty of amiable friends. He had a daily round that was quite devoid of hardship. All morning he would work at his desk, as steadily and busily as a bookkeeper. When he finished one composition he would start another, sometimes on the same page. Most men, completing so formidable a thing as a string quartette, are exhausted, and have to resort to drink, travel, politics or religion for recuperation. But not Schubert. He simply began an opera or a mass.

At 1 o'clock or thereabout he would knock off for the day and go to dinner at a restaurant, usually the one called "Zum Roten Kreuz"—the Red Cross. It was a cheap place, but the food was good and the beer was better. Like most bachelors, Schubert never dined alone. There were always agreeable companions, mainly young musicians like himself. They would remain at table for hours and then Schubert would take a walk. In the evening he and his brothers and their friends made music. They started with a little family orchestra but it grew so large that the family home could not contain it, and it moved to the larger house of an acquaintance. It played almost every night. Schubert usually played the viola, but sometimes he was the pianist.

This was his routine from October to June. In summer he wandered about the Danubian countryside, usually with a friend or two. They were always welcome, and had many more invitations than they could accept. They would go to this or that country house, stay a week, and enchant the family and other guests with their music. Schubert would often write something for the occasion. It was thus that he produced his superb setting to Shakespeare's "Who is Sylvia?" It was thus that he wrote most of his German dances —waltzes and *Ländler*. He composed a great many more of these dances than he ever put on paper. He would sit at the piano and they would flow from his fingers by the hour.

Those that survive are all very beautiful. Schubert thus had little need for money, and hence made an easy mark for the music publishers. He sold some of his songs to them for as little as 20 cents. Now and then, pulling himself together, he resolved to make a stake, and usually, on such occasions, he wrote an opera. But his operas were always failures, and most of them never got to the stage. A successful opera composer is half musician and half clown; sometimes the clown part of him is two-thirds, or even nine-tenths. Schubert had no talent in that direction. He was an artist, not a showman.

Much of his best music he never heard played, save by the family orchestra. This was true even of his Unfinished Symphony, one of the noblest works in the whole range of music. He wrote the two movements that we have six years before his death, but then abandoned it, and it did not become generally known until long afterward. His great C Major fared even more badly. In 1844 the London Philharmonic put it into rehearsal, but the members of the orchestra, for some unknown reason, laughed at it, and it was shelved until 1856. After Schubert's death so many of his unpublished songs began to appear that many persons suspected his brother Ferdinand of forging them.

But Schubert, in life, wasted little time worrying about the fate of his music. He wrote it, not to entertain concert audiences, but to please himself, and out of that fact flowed a great deal of its magnificent merit. It is, in large part, so familiar to the musicians of today that they often overlook its astounding orginality. Not infrequently one

finds anticipations in it—even of Wagner!—but it is almost wholly bare of reminiscence. Schubert's harmonies
were unlike the harmonies of any composer who had gone
before him. They were not only different; they were better.
His melodies differed enormously from those of his fore-
runners. He did not look back to Mozart and Haydn: he
looked forward to Brahms. Maybe Beethoven influenced
him. There are, indeed, indications that way in the Tragic
Symphony, written in 1816, and especially in the slow
movement. But Beethoven would have been proud of that
slow movement if he had written it himself—and it remains, in the last analysis, pure Schubert. No one else,
before or since, could have done it.

As I have said, Schubert led a placid and care-free life.
Now and then he was on short commons, and had to double
up in lodgings with a friend or two, but that was no hardship for a young bachelor. He knew a great many pleasant
people, male and female, and they admired him and made
much of him. The gals were not unappreciative of him,
though he was surely no beauty. He loved good wine and
got down many a carboy of it in his time. Vienna was gay
and charming, even when there was war—and the war was
over before he was nineteen.

Nevertheless, such stray confidences as we have from
him indicates that he was given to melancholy and often
fell into cruel depressions. His music, he once wrote in a
diary, came out of the depth of his sorrow. The fact is written all over it. It is very seldom merry. Schubert wrote some
of the most dark and somber music ever written—for ex-

ample the "Winterreise" cycle, the last movement of the Unfinished, the slow movement of the Tragic, the first movement of the quintette with the two 'cellos, and such songs as the familiar Serenade. Even his *scherzi* tend to be gloomy, as witness the two in the octette.

Love? Heartache? A haughty wench? Hardly. Schubert's contemporaries heard of nothing of the sort. To them he was simply *Schwammerl*, a care-free and charming fellow, handy with the girls and a capital companion at the *Biertisch*. They forgot, seeing him every day, that he was also an artist—one of the greatest, indeed, ever known in the world. They forgot that an artist forges his work out of inner substance by a process almost cannibalistic—that the price of beauty is heavy striving and cruel pain—that all artists, at bottom, are forlorn and melancholy men. They had Beethoven before them, wracked and consumed by his own vapors, but they were too close to Schubert to see into him.

Thus artists pay for what they give us. Schubert got off easily. He was dead at 32, and behind him trailed a series of almost incomparable masterpieces. His genius was of the first caliber. Dead a hundred years, he remains as alive as the child born yesterday. Out of his dark moods came treasures that belong to all of us. He increased the stature and dignity of man. He was one of the truly great men.

Schubert

From the *American Mercury*, November, 1928, pp. 284–6.
Included in A MENCKEN CHRESTOMATHY, 1949, pp. 527–32.

FRANZ SCHUBERT, at least in Anglo-Saxondom, has evaded
the indignity of too much popularity. Even his lovely "Serenade," perhaps the most moving love-song ever written, has
escaped being mauled at weddings in the manner of Mendelssohn's march from "A Midsummer Night's Dream"
and Wagner's from "Lohengrin." It is familiar, but not
thread-bare; I have listened to it within the past week with
new delight in its noble and poignant melody, its rhythmic
and harmonic ingenuity, its indescribable Schubertian flavor. Nor is there anything stale about nine-tenths of his
piano music, or the songs. The former is played very little
—far, far too little. The latter are yowled in all the music
studios of the world, but the populace remains unaware of
them, and so they manage to hold their dignity and charm.
"The Erl King" and "Who is Sylvia?" have become familiar
on the air, but surely not many of the remaining six hundred.

Schubert, indeed, was far too fine an artist to write for
the mob. When he tried to do it in the theater he failed
miserably, and more than once he even failed in the concert-hall. There is the case, for example, of "Heidenröslein",
to Goethe's words. Goethe wrote them in 1773 and
J. F. Reichardt set them in 1793. In 1815, a year after
Reichardt's death, Schubert made a new setting. Was it
better—that is, considering the homely words? No; it was

harder to sing, but not better. Twleve years later the text was reset again by Heinrich Werner, a composer so obscure that even Grove's Dictionary is silent about him, but a man, obviously, with all the gift for simple, transparent melody of a Friedrich Silcher. When "Heidenröslein" is sung today it is to Werner's melody, not Schubert's.

Great stretches of Schubert's music, indeed, remain almost unknown, even to musicians. Perhaps a hundred of his songs are heard regularly in the concert-hall; the rest get upon programmes only rarely. Of his chamber music little is heard at all, not even the two superb piano trios, the octet, and the quintet with the two 'cellos. Of his symphonies the orchestras play the Unfinished incessantly— but never too often!—and the huge C Major now and then, but the Tragic only once in a blue moon. Yet the Tragic remains one of Schubert's masterworks, and in its slow movement, at least, it rises to the full height of the Unfinished. There are not six such slow movements in the whole range of music. It has an eloquence that has never been surpassed, not even by Beethoven, but there is no rhetoric in it, no heroics, no exhibitionism. It begins quietly and simply and it passes out in a whisper, but its beauty remains overwhelming. I defy anyone with ears to listen to it without being moved profoundly, as by the spectacle of great grief.

We know little directly about what Schubert thought of his compositions. He was, for a musician, strangely reserved. But indirectly there is the legend that, in his last days, he thought of taking lessons in counterpoint from

Simon Sechter. The story has always appealed pleasantly to the musical biographers; mainly ninth-rate men, they delight in discovering imbecilities in artists. My guess is that Schubert, if he actually proposed to seek the den of Sechter, did it in a sportive spirit. Going to school to a pedant would have appealed charmingly to his sardonic humor. What Sechter had to teach him was precisely what a Hugh Walpole might have taught Joseph Conrad, no less and no more.

It is astonishing how voluptuously criticism cherishes nonsense. This notion that Schubert lacked skill at counterpoint seems destined to go on afflicting his fame forever, despite the plain evidence to the contrary in his most familiar works. How can anyone believe it who has so much as glanced at the score of the Unfinished? That score is quite as remarkable for its adroit and lovely combinations of melodies as it is for its magnificent modulations. It is seldom that one is heard alone. They come in two by two, and they are woven into a fabric that is at once simple and complicated, and always beautiful. Here is contrapuntal writing at its very best, for the means are concealed by a perfect effect. Here is the complete antithesis of the sort of counterpoint that is taught by the Sechters.

No doubt the superstition that Schubert had no skill at polyphony gets some support from the plain fact that he seldom wrote a formal fugue. There is one at the end of his cantata, "Miriam's Siegesgesang", and in his last year he wrote another for piano duet. The strict form however, was out of accord with the natural bent of his invention; he did not think of terse, epigrammatic subjects, as Bach did and Beethoven afterward; he thought of complete melodies, the most ravishing ever heard in this world. It would be hard to imagine his making anything of the four austere notes which Beethoven turned into the first movement of the C minor symphony. He would have gone on to develop them melodically before ever he set himself to manipulating them contrapuntally. But that was not a sign of his inferiority to Beethoven; it was, in its way, a sign of his superiority. He was infinitely below old Ludwig as a technician; he lacked the sheer brain-power that went into such masterpieces as the first movement of the Eroica and the *allegretto* of the Seventh. Such dizzy feats of pure craftsmanship were beyond him. But where he fell short as an artisan he was unsurpassed as an artist. He invented more beautiful musical ideas in his thirty-one years than even Mozart or Haydn, and he proclaimed them with an instinctive skill that was certainly not inferior to any mere virtuosity, however dazzling and however profound.

This instinctive skill is visible quite as clearly in his counterpoint as it is in his harmony. Throwing off the pedantic fetters that bound even Bach, he got into polyphony all the ease and naturalness of simple melody. His subjects and counter-subjects are never tortured to meet the rules; they flow on with a grace like that of wheat rippled by the wind. The defect of prettiness is not in them. They show, at their most trivial, all the fine dignity of Schubert the man. Beautiful always in their simple statement, they take on fresh and even more enchanting beauties when one supports another. There are passages in the Unfinished, especially in the first movement, that are almost unparalleled in music, and there are passages equally fine in compositions that are seldom heard, notably the aforesaid quintet. When Schubert died the art of writing so magnificently seemed to pass out of the world. It was not until the colossal figure of Brahms arose that it found another master.

He was, to music, its great heart, as Beethoven was its great mind. All the rest begin to seem a bit archaic, but he continues to be a contemporary. He was essentially a modern, though he was born in the Eighteenth Century. In his earliest compositions there was something far beyond the naïve idiom of Mozart and Haydn. Already in "The Erl King" there was an echo of Beethoven's fury; later on it was to be transformed into a quieter mood, but one none the less austere. The man lived his inner life upon a high level. Outwardly a simple and unpretentious fellow, and condemned by poverty to an uneventful routine, he yet walked with the gods. His contacts with the world brought him only defeat and dismay. He failed at all the enterprises whereby the musicians of his day got fame and money. But out of every failure there flowed a masterpiece.

In all the history of music there has never been another man of such stupendous natural talents. It would be difficult, indeed, to match him in any of the other fine arts. He was the artist *par excellence*, moved by a powerful instinct to create beauty, and equipped by a prodigal nature with the precise and perfect tools. The gabble about his defective training probably comes down to us from his innocent friends and fellows in Vienna. They never estimated him at his true stature, but they at least saw that there was something extraordinary and even miraculous about him— that what he did could not be accounted for logically, but lay far beyond the common bounds of cause and effect. We know next to nothing about his mental processes. He was surrounded by inferiorities who noted with wonder how savagely he worked, how many hours a day he put in at his writing-table, and what wonders he achieved, but were too dull to be interested in what went on inside his head. Schubert himself was silent on that subject. From him there issued not even the fragmentary revelations that came from Mozart. All we know is that his ideas flowed like a cataract —that he knew nothing of Beethoven's tortured wooing of beauty—that his first thoughts, more often than not, were complete, perfect and incomparable.

No composer of the first rank has failed to surpass him in this way or that, but he stands above all of them as a contriver of sheer beauty, as a maker of music in the purest sense. There is no more smell of the lamp in his work than there is in the lyrics of Shakespeare. It is infinitely artless and spontaneous. But in its artlessness there is no sign of that intellectual poverty which so often shows itself, for example, in Haydn. Few composers, not even Beethoven and Bach, have been so seldom banal. He can be repetitious and even tedious, but it seems a sheer impossibility for him to be obvious or hollow. Such defects get into works of art when the composer's lust to create is unaccompanied by a sufficiency of sound and charming ideas. But Schubert never lacked ideas. Within the limits of his interests and curiosities he hatched more good ideas in his thirty-one years than all the rest of mankind has hatched since the beginning of time.

Music is kind to its disciples. When they bring high talents to its service they are not forgotten. They survive among the durably salient men, the really great men, the remembered men. Schubert belongs in that rare and enviable company. Life used him harshly, but time has made up for it. He is one of the great glories of the human race.

◆◆◆◆◆◆◆◆◆◆

Wagner

(1 8 1 3 – 8 3)

SYMBIOSIS AND THE ARTIST

From *Toward a Realistic Æsthetic*, PREJUDICES: FOURTH
SERIES, 1924, pp. 249–51.
First printed in the *Smart Set*, July, 1922, pp. 41–3.
Included in A MENCKEN CHRESTOMATHY, 1949, pp. 536–7.

IN CONTEMPLATING the stupendous achievements of Wagner one finds one's self wondering how much further he would have gone had he not been harassed by his two dreadful wives. The first, Minna Planer, was implacably opposed to his life-work, and made hard efforts to dissuade him from it. She regarded "Lohengrin" as nonsensical and "Tannhäuser" as downright indecent. It was her constant hope, until Wagner finally kicked her out, that he would give over such stuff, and consecrate himself to the composition of respectable operas in the manner of Rossini. She was a singer, and had the brains of one. It must be plain that the presence of such a woman—and Wagner lived with her for twenty years—must have put a fearful burden upon his creative genius. No man can be absolutely indifferent to the opinions and prejudices of his wife. She has too many opportunities to shove them down his throat. If she can't make him listen to them by howling and bawling, she can make him listen by snuffling. To say that he can carry on his work without paying any heed to her is equal to saying that he can carry on his work without paying any heed to his toothache, his conscience, or the zoo next door. In spite of Minna, Wagner composed a number of very fine music dramas. But if he had poisoned her at the beginning of his career it is very likely that he could have composed more of them, and perhaps better ones.

His second wife, the celebrated Cosima Liszt-von Bülow, had far more intelligence than Minna, and so we may assume that her presence in his music factory was less of a handicap upon the composer. Nevertheless, the chances are that she, too, did him far more harm than good. To begin with, she was extremely plain in face—and nothing is more damaging to the creative faculty than the constant presence of ugliness. Cosima, in fact, looked not unlike a modern woman politician; even Nietzsche, a very romantic young fellow, had to go crazy before he could fall in love with her. In the second place, there is good reason to believe that

Cosima, until Wagner's death, secretly believed that her father, Papa Liszt, was a far better musician. Men's wives almost invariably make some such mistake; to find one who can separate the man of genius from the mere husband, and then estimate the former accurately and fairly, is surely very rare. A woman usually respects her father, but her view of her husband is mingled with contempt, for she is of course privy to the transparent devices by which she snared him. It is difficult for her, being so acutely aware of the weakness of the man, to give due weight to the dignity of the artist. Moreover, Cosima had shoddy tastes, and they played destructively upon poor Wagner. There are parts of "Parsifal" that suggest her very strongly—far more strongly, in fact, than they suggest the author of "Die Meistersinger."

I do not here decry Wagner; on the contrary, I praise him, and perhaps excessively. It is staggering to think of the work he did, with Minna and Cosima shrilling in his ears. What interests me is the question as to how much further he might have gone had he escaped the passionate affection of the two of them and of their various volunteer assistants. The thought fascinates, and almost alarms. There is a limit beyond which sheer beauty becomes unseemly. In "Tristan und Isolde", in the "Ring", and even in parts of "Parsifal", Wagner pushes his music very near that limit. A bit beyond lies the fourth dimension of tone—and madness.

Wagner

THE ETERNAL FARCE

From *Reflections on Human Monogamy*,
PREJUDICES: FOURTH SERIES, 1924, pp. 107–8.
First printed in the *Smart Set*, March, 1922, p. 44.
Included in A MENCKEN CHRESTOMATHY, 1949, pp. 537–8.

EVEN NIETZSCHE was deceived by Wagner's "Parsifal."
Like the most maudlin German fat woman at Bayreuth,
he mistook the composer's elaborate and outrageous burlesque of Christianity for a tribute to Christianity, and so
denounced him as a jackass and refused to speak to him
thereafter. To this day "Parsifal" is given with all the trap-
pings of a religious ceremonial, and pious folks go to hear
it who would instantly shut their ears if the band began
playing "Tristan und Isolde." It has become, in fact, a sort
of "Way Down East" or "Ben-Hur" of music drama—a
bait for luring patrons who are never seen in the opera house
otherwise. But try to imagine such a thumping atheist as
Wagner writing a religious opera seriously! And if, by any
chance, you succeed in imagining it, then turn to the Char-
Freitag music, and play it on your phonograph. Here is the
central scene of the piece, the moment of most austere
solemnity—and to it Wagner fits music that is so luscious
and so fleshy—indeed, so downright lascivious and indecent—that even I, who am almost anesthetic to such provo-
cations, blush every time I hear it. The Flower Maidens
do not raise my blood-pressure a single ohm; I have actually
drowsed through the whole second act of "Tristan." But

when I hear that Char-Freitag music all my Freudian suppressions begin groaning and stretching their legs in the dungeons of my unconscious. And what does Char-Freitag mean? Char-Freitag means Good Friday!

❖❖❖❖❖❖❖❖❖❖

Franz Joseph Haydn

(1732–1809)

From the Baltimore *Evening Sun*, November 23, 1916.

(The following article [Franz Joseph Haydn] is one of a number written by Mencken to encourage interest in the newly created Baltimore Symphony Orchestra. It was the first instance in this country that an orchestra was entirely subsidized by the city government. Dr. Gustav Strube, assistant conductor of the Boston Symphony Orchestra, was brought to Baltimore to be its conductor.)

NEVER HAVING HEARD the Haydn symphony which Dr. Strube and his tone artists are to perform on Friday night, I am unable to tell you precisely what is in it, but all the same I offer my ears in wager that good stuff is there, and that no one will hear it without joy. Old Haydn wrote so many symphonies that no one in the world has heard them all, but he never wrote one that lacked beauty, and he never wrote one that was not marked all over by his extraordinarily cheerful and ingratiating personality. Exploring them is an almost endless business and full of charming surprises. Some time ago, idling away a half hour at Schirmer's I happened upon one so crowded with loveliness that its relative obscurity remains astounding. A composition of such unusual beauties written today, would make a composer's reputation. But Haydn wrote dozens, nay scores, like it: and many of them are now moldering on the shelf and forgotten by all save compilers of thematic catalogues. Beethoven stopped with nine symphonies; Mozart with forty;[1] Schumann and Brahms with four each; Schubert with eight; Tschaikowsky with six; Mendelssohn with five; Mahler with eight or nine. But Haydn wrote fully a hundred, not counting symphonic overtures, and among them all it is difficult to find a dull one, or one which does not show superb musicianship on every page.

The very clarity and simplicity of these great works has mitigated against a true understanding of their merit. Too often they are dismissed as hollow, as trivial, almost as infantile. In the shadow of the vast compositions of Beethoven they shrink to almost nothing. But a diligent study of them is all that is needed to rehabilitate them. Under the smooth and glistening surface there is seen a structure of the utmost complexity and ingenuity. They are magnificently articulated and thought out. They stand as unsurpassable examples of that exact and inevitable form which is the soul of all great music. There are ideas in them; the flow of beautiful sound never ceases for an instant; they have a beginning, a middle and an end; they hang together almost perfectly. One turns to them, from harmonic and emotional bombastics of modern orchestral music. . . .

But Haydn was more than a great composer of music;

[1] Actually, Mozart wrote 41 symphonies, Haydn 104.

he was, beyond everything else, a great musical revolutionary. The orchestra as we know it today is his creation, or, at any rate, more his than any other man's. He put form and logic into the symphony, the most formal and logical of musical forms. He improved and gave direction to the solo sonata. Above all, he left the marks of his genius upon the string quartet. His principal quartets, even after all these years, remain fresh and vigorous; they still dispute for places on programs with the quartets of Beethoven and the vastly more complex quartets of a later day. In them, and for the first time, one finds that varied and resourceful four-part writing which is the secret of all the charm of the form, and that adroit use of polyphony which alone makes it possible. And in them, too, despite many a naïf touch, one finds a sound understanding of the capabilities and limitations of the four instruments, and an amazing skill at developing their beauties. The famous Kaiser quartet, as it stands, is so nearly perfect that the search for flaws in it can only lead to absurdity. Beethoven, true enough, wrote greater quartets, but he surely never wrote a greater one within those limits.

As for the symphonies, they are little heard today, not so much because they are empty of the wild emotion that music-lovers have been taught to look for, as because they are infernally difficult of execution. Their very simplicity, in fact, is what makes them hard to play properly; the slightest error in tone or dynamics sticks out like a sore thumb. Modern music, by its bewildering complexity, gives tone artists hedges to hide behind. Once in Munich, hearing

"Electra" from the front row of the orchestra, I observed several of the first violins lose their places. A kindly brother in art hauled them up by stabbing them in the ribs with his fiddle bow. But though they had been playing *fortissimo*, it made not the slightest difference to the audience, and even the conductor was unaware of their mishap. A musician lately told me of a similar proceeding, deliberate this time, in the Boston Symphony Orchestra. During the performance of a celebrated tone-poem, much disliked by the men, a group of the first violins invariably played *"Fuchs, du hast die Gans Gestolen"*, or some other such sweet lullaby. But the audience never noticed it, and neither did Dr. Fiedler, the estimable *kapellmeister* . . . imagine that sort of thing in Haydn! The very ushers would scream! [2]

Haydn was born in 1732 at Rohrau, a small town in Austria, near the border of Hungary. His father was the village blacksmith, and also practiced the science of a church sexton; his mother had been third cook in the household of Graf Harrach, a local magnifico. Mamma Haydn had 12 little Haydns, and after her death her successor had 5 more. Joseph was the second of the 17. At the age of 6 he was humanely rescued from this happy home by an uncle from the nearby town of Hainsburg, one Johann

[2] These are not exaggerations. The concert-master of the Baltimore Symphony Orchestra, beside whom I played as assistant, frequently improvised variations on "Dixie" during rehearsals and even performances of contemporary compositions for which he did not care, unnoticed under the very nose of one of our later conductors.

Matthias Frankh, a schoolmaster. Uncle Johann taught him the violin and harpsichord and discovered that he had a voice. One day this voice was heard by George Reutter, the court *kapellmeister* at Vienna, and in 1740 little Joseph was translated to the capital, where he was soon piping a shrill soprano in the choir of Old Steffel, the Vienna cathedral, and taking lessons from two professors named Gegenbauer and Finsterbusch. Of Gegenbauer and Finsterbusch nothing more is known; they fade from the chronicle like Rosenkranz and Guildenstern.

Joseph, his voice having broken, was kicked out of the choir in 1749, and for two or three years thereafter he led a very lonely and miserable life, and came near starving. Only one person seems to have genuinely befriended him, a storekeeper named Buchholz. This Buchholz, on no security save his belief in the boy's genius, lent him 150 florins—a very large sum for those days. Years afterward, in his will, Haydn left the daughter of Buchholz 100 florins in memory of her father's generosity. Buchholz himself had been repaid 50 years before and was long since dead. Haydn never forgot such kindnesses. His will, indeed, mentioned everyone who had been kind to him during his long life, including especially Johann Frankh, and he left substantial bequests to the children of all of them. Fully 50 persons were mentioned by name in this testament, ranging from the son of that Graf von Harrach for whom Haydn's mother had worked as a cook, to the composer's old body-servant Johann Elssler, to whom he left money enough to keep him at ease for the rest of his days.

It was Metastasio the poet who first set Haydn on his legs. How they met is not known, but Metastasio got him a pupil in Senorita Marianne von Martinez, a daughter to the Master of Ceremonies to the Papal Nuncio, and this connection brought him to the notice of various influential persons, and after engagements as orchestral conductor with Baron von Fürnberg, Countess von Thun, Count Hagwitz, Count Morzin and other members of the nobility, he began that long engagement with the Esterhazys which was to make his reputation and his fortune, and to color the whole stream of his life. The Prince Esterhazy of that time was Paul Anton, and like all his relatives he was an ardent musician. The family castle at Eisenstadt, in the Hungarian mountains, had always had a private orchestra: before the end of Haydn's 30 years of service this orchestra was to be increased to 45 men, and to become an organization of the highest consequence. The Esterhazys had plenty of money to pay for such luxuries. Among them they possessed 29 titles of nobility, and owned 21 castles, 60 market towns and 414 villages in Hungary alone, not to mention vast estates in Lower Austria and a whole county in Bavaria. At Eisenstadt, though it was remote and lonely, Haydn was very happy, for he had a patron who was eager to help him and he had an orchestra for all his experiments. Here, and later at Esterhaz, he learned to write music by writing it; here he tried out the plans that were to revolutionize music; here he composed most of his immortal works.

Much has been made of Haydn's so-called servile position

at Eisenstadt and Esterhaz. It is commonly believed, indeed, that his rank was that of a servant, and that he was compelled to eat in the kitchen. Pious articles without number have been written upon his woes, upon the insults he suffered, upon his humility under them. Much poppycock is here covered with moralizing sugar. The truth is that Haydn was anything but a shrinking and humble fellow. He was a great artist and he knew it, and you may be sure that he exacted the politeness due his character, even from so powerful a family of magnates as the Esterhazys. Moreover, the text of his contract with Prince Paul Anton, published in J. Cuthbert Haddon's life, shows plainly that he was not ranked as a servant at all, but that it was provided that he should be "considered and treated as a member of the household", that he should be considered an "Official", and that he should mess with the officers of the Prince's staff. In brief, his footing was exactly that of the minor nobles who surrounded the great and powerful Prince, and what is more, he got a good salary for those times. Toward the end of his service he received 1,400 florins a year, his board and lodging, and a liberal allowance for clothes and traveling expenses. This, in the money of today, was equal to the pay and allowances of a lieutenant in the navy.

Prince Paul Anton died a year after Haydn got to Eisenstadt and was succeeded by his brother Nicolaus, a gaudy and Gargantuan personage. Nicolaus was the Diamond Jim Brady of his time. He spent his immense revenues upon gigantic fetes and shows, and wore uniforms heavily encrusted with precious stones. His notion of a good time was to go boar-hunting with a hundred companions, and then feast and carouse for two weeks. Nevertheless the family love of music was in him, and he seems to have treated Haydn with great respect. Not content with having music made for him, he essayed to make it himself, and so spent his rainy days practicing on the violoncello and the barytone, a somewhat smaller instrument of the same tribe, now happily extinct. Haydn wrote no fewer than 175 compositions for the barytone, including three concertos, and Nicolaus played them all. On this instrument, perhaps, the Prince was a competent performer, but he seems to have had difficulties with the 'cello, for in all of Haydn's trios the parts for it are very simple, and there is a legend that he made them so in order to please his patron. These trios suffer from the fact to this day, for 'cellists dislike them, and so their great beauties are seldom heard. Haydn himself played either the violin or the clavier parts: both are difficult and intensely interesting.

As I have said, Haydn remained with the Esterhazys, off and on for 30 years. Then he went to England as Händel had done before him. He was received with the highest respect when he got there, and became, indeed, the chief lion of London, but it took a lot of arguing to induce him to go. On the one hand, he was getting old and greatly disliked travel; on the other hand, he had many ties in Vienna. One hears of him struggling painfully with the English language, and longing sadly for the flesh-pots of Wien. The English victualry did not please him; he would awake in the night weeping for a basin of German *Linsensuppe* and a slab of the excellent coffee cake of his old friend Frau von Genziger. Worse, a widow of London, Mrs. Schroeter, tried to ensnare him, despite the fact that he was married. (He had been separated from his wife, a barber's daughter for 23 years.) All in all he longed to escape, and in 1792 he returned home. But two years later he was lured back and remained until the summer of 1795. Despite his discomforts, he wrote some of his best music in England, including half a dozen symphonies.[3]

Back in Austria once more, he devoted himself wholeheartedly to composition, and among the fruits of his last years were "The Creation", "The Seasons" and the Austrian national anthem, now universally known as "Deutschland über Alles." The last named is, by all odds, the most beautiful of all national anthems, and the most respectable as music. Haydn wrote it to order. Austria, at that time, had no national hymn, and the Imperial Chancellor, Graf von Saurau, engaged the poet Ilaschka to write one. (The original words, "Gott erhalte Franz den Kaiser" are still used by the Austrians.) Haydn was then invited to provide music for it, and one of his characteristic inspirations gave him the lovely melody now so familiar. When the hymn was first sung on February 12, 1797, it made a colossal success, and Haydn became a national idol.

The composer himself ranked his hymn above all his other compositions. When the French bombarded Vienna in 1809 he seated himself at his piano every morning and

[3] Actually Haydn composed twelve symphonies in London—probably his very best—six in 1791 and another six in 1794.

played the melody amid the booming of the guns. In May of that year, only five days before his death, he arose from his bed and played it three times in succession. The air had acquired a lofty sacredness in his eyes. He was a firm patriot and its adoption by his people had moved him profoundly.

❖❖❖❖❖❖❖❖❖❖

Johann Strauss

(1 8 2 5 – 9 9)

From the Chicago *Tribune*, December 13, 1925.
Also from *Five Little Excursions*,
Prejudices: sixth series, 1927, pp. 169–74.
Included in A Mencken Chrestomathy, 1949, pp. 538–41.

The centenary of Johann Strauss the Younger in 1925 passed almost unnoticed in the United States. In Berlin and in Vienna it was celebrated with imposing ceremonies, and all the German radio stations put "Wein, Weib und Gesang" and "Rosen aus dem Süden" on the air. Why wasn't it done in this great country? Was the curse of jazz to blame —or was it due to the current pestilence of Prohibition and the consequent scarcity of sound beer? I incline to Answer No. 2. Any music is difficult on well-water, but the waltz is a sheer impossibility. "Man Lebt Nur Einmal" is as dreadful in a dry country as a Sousa march at a hanging.

For the essence of a Viennese waltz, and especially of a Strauss waltz, is merriment, good humor, happiness. Sad music, to be sure, has been written in Vienna—but chiefly

Plate IV · *Mask and music in the brick garden wall built by Mencken, in the back yard of his home on Hollins Street. The mask of Beethoven's head and the opening motif of the Fifth Symphony were cast in concrete by his brother, August*

PLATE V · *Mencken (on the left) singing with a quartet from the press-room and composing-room to the children of war correspondents at a Christmas party, Sun office, December 22, 1944*

by foreigners: Haydn, who was a Croat; Beethoven, whose pap had been a sour Rhine wine; Brahms, who came from the bleak Baltic coast. I came upon Schubert—but all the rules go to pot when he appears. As for Strauss, he was 100% Viennese, and could no more be sad than he could be indignant. The waltz wandered into the minor keys in Paris, in the hands of the sardonic Alsatian Jew, Waldteufel, but at home old Johann kept it in golden major, and so did young Johann after him. The two, taking it from Schubert and the folk, lifted it to imperial splendor. No other dance-form, not even the minuet, has ever brought forth more lovely music. And none other has preserved so perfectly the divine beeriness of the peasant dance. The best of the Strauss waltzes were written for the most stilted and cere-monious court in Europe, but in every one of them, great and little, there remains the boggy, expansive flavor of the village green. Even the stately "Kaiser" waltz, with its pre-liminary heelclicks and saber-rattling, is soon swinging jocosely to the measures of the rustic *Springtanz*.

It is a curious, melancholy and gruesome fact that Jo-hann Strauss II was brought up to the variety of delinquency known as investment banking. His father planned that he should be what in our time is called a bond salesman. What asses fathers are. This one was himself a great master of the waltz, and yet he believed that he could save all three of his sons from its lascivious allurement. Young Johann was dedi-cated to investment banking, Josef to architecture, and Eduard, the baby, to the law. The old man died on Septem-ber 25, 1849. On September 26 all three were writing waltzes. Johann, it quickly appeared, was the best of the trio. In fact, he was the best musician who ever wrote waltzes for dancing, and one of the salient composers of all time. He took the waltz as his father left it, and gradually built it up into a form almost symphonic. He developed the introduction, which had been little more than an opening fanfare, into a complex and beautiful thing, almost an overture, and he elaborated the coda until it began to demand every resource of the composer's art, including even counterpoint. And into the waltz itself he threw such melodic riches, so vastly a rhythmic inventiveness and so adept a mastery of instrumentation that the effect was overwhelming. The Strauss waltzes, it seems to me, have never been sufficiently studied. Consider, for example, the astonishing skill with which Johann manages his procession of keys—the inevitable air which he always gets into his choice. And the immense ingenuity with which he puts variety into his bass—so monotonous in Waldteufel, and even in Lanner and Gung'l. And the endless resourcefulness which marks his orchestration—never formal and obvious for an instant, but always with some new quirk in it, some fresh and charming beauty. And his codas—how simple they are, and yet how ravishing. Johann certainly did not blush unseen. He was an important figure at the Austrian court, and when he passed necks were craned as if at an ambassador. He traveled widely and was received with honor everywhere. His waltzes swept the world. His operettas, following them, offered formidable rivalry to the pieces of Gilbert and

Sullivan. He was plastered with orders. He took in, in his time, a great deal of money, and left all his wives well provided for. More, he had the respect and a little of the envy of all his musical contemporaries. Wagner delighted in his waltzes and so did Brahms. Once one of the Strauss wives, encountering Brahms at the annual ball of the Third Assembly District Democratic Association of Vienna, asked him to sign her fan. He wrote upon it the opening theme of "The Beautiful Blue Danube" and added "Leider nicht von Johannes Brahms"—Unfortunately, not by Johannes Brahms. It was a compliment indeed—perhaps the most tremendous recorded in history—nor was there any mere politeness in it, for Brahms had written plenty of waltzes himself, and knew it was not as easy as it looked.

The lesser fish followed the whales. There was never any clash of debate over Strauss. It was unanimously agreed that he was first-rate. His field was not wide, but within that field he was unchallenged. He became, in the end, the dean of a sort of college of waltz writers, centering in Vienna. The waltz, as he had brought it up to perfection, became the standard ball-room dance of the civilized world, and though it had to meet rivals constantly, it held its own for two generations, and even now, despite the murrain of jazz, it comes back once more. Disciples of great skill began to appear in the Straussian wake—Ziehrer with the beautiful "Weaner Mad'l", Komchak with "Fidelis Wien", Lincke with "Ach, Frühling, Wie Bist Du So Schön", and many another. But the old Johann never lost his primacy. Down to the very day of his death in 1899 he was *primus inter omnes.* Vienna wept oceans of beery tears into his grave. A great Viennese—perhaps the ultimate flower of old Vienna —was gone.

◇◇◇◇◇◇◇◇◇◇◇

Schumann

(1 8 1 0 – 5 6)

O, Fruehling, Wie Bist Du So Schoen!
From the Baltimore *Evening Sun*, April 13, 1916.

ROBERT SCHUMANN's Symphony No. 1, in B flat, which Mr. Strube and his band are to play on Friday night, contains more of pure joy, it is likely, than any other symphonic work in the classical repertoire, saving only Beethoven's No. 8. And no wonder! It was written under conditions that would have inflamed even a prohibitionist to happiness. Schumann was young, he had just made his first big successes, such men as Liszt and Moscheles were beginning to notice him, he was well-to-do and in good health, he was making his first serious venture in the enticing field of the grand orchestra, it was a glorious German Springtime— and he was in the midst of his honeymoon with his lovely and talented wife, the inspiration of all that was best in him and the idol of his heart to the end of his days. Picture the scene, the situation. And then go to hear the symphony!

Schumann was married to Clara Wieck on September 12,

1840, exactly 40 years to a day, by the way, before Christendom was adorned by [4]—but let it pass! He began work on the symphony in February, 1841, and on a day, as we learn from a letter to Karl Taubert, when the first breath of spring was in the air. It was his original intention to call it "A Spring Symphony", and the first and last movements, in manuscript, were labeled "Spring's Awakening" and "Spring's Farewell", respectively; but when the time came to publish it he decided to let it go out without any program. In truth, it needs none. No one with the slightest imagination can hear it without sensing its significance. From the opening blare of the trumpets and French horns to the final chords for full orchestra, the triumphant gayety of Springtime is in it. It is full of arch and tickling passages. Its melodies are sparkling, and chase one another in and out. Schumann kicks up his legs, and takes deep breaths of the vernal air, and praises God with happy tunes. As I have said, the work was the fruit of the composer's first serious effort to write for grand orchestra. He had attempted a symphony, true enough, in 1830, but he was then only 20 years old and it was so bad that it remained unpublished, and is still, in fact, in manuscript. His symphony in B flat was thus his initial essay in writing for the whole band, and naturally enough he did not master the difficult technique of that enterprise at one stroke. When the work was first played the opening measures, being ineptly scored for the horns, sounded so badly that the audience laughed, and Schumann at once raised the whole passage a third, in which form it

[4] Henry Mencken was born on September 12, 1880.

appears now. There were other rough spots in the original score, and the composer changed some of them when the symphony was done in Leipzig. These blemishes, no doubt, set going the notion still held by many critics, that Schumann was a bad writer for the orchestra. In this notion there is some truth, for he was a composer for the piano first of all, and many of his orchestral works give the impression of having been conceived for the piano and then scored, but there is so much of pure beauty in them that we can well forgive an occasional slip. Schumann was never a great master of the orchestral idiom, like Wagner, Berlioz and Richard Strauss, but he wrote competently enough, after all, to make his ideas clear, and those ideas were always supremely well worth hearing. In his four symphonies one finds some of the most magnificent symphonic music written since Beethoven. It belongs to an altogether higher range than the music of his old rival, Mendelssohn, and stands plainly above the sonorous but maudlin stuff of such fellows as Tschaikovsky. Here, however, comparisons begin to grow difficult, for the symphony has undergone great changes in late years, and it would be impossible to undertake any intelligible choice between the Schumann symphonies and the huge orchestral works of Strauss and Mahler. When it comes to Brahms—but let us avoid trouble by forgetting old Johannes. The Spring Symphony, as I have twice remarked, opens with a rousing theme for trumpet and French Horns, the which is at once repeated by the full orchestra *fortissimo*. It is, as Schumann himself said, the call of Spring, the summons to be up and cavorting. A fiery passage follows, with the fiddles squeaking high up on the E string, and the 'cellos and bull-fiddles haw-hawing far below. Pan is loose; the woods are awakening. Then comes, very softly, a fragmentary restatement of the trumpet theme, this time for wood-wind, and then a cadenza-like solo passage for the first flute, and a sudden hurrying of the tempo. A few measures further on the introduction glides beautifully into the first movement proper. It opens with a gay theme made of the trumpet call, and to the tail of it is hooked a rustling passage for the strings, delightfully suggestive of the breeze blowing through greening trees. The second subject, first given out by the clarinets and bassoons and kept in the wood-wind throughout the movement, is a simple and plaintive song, but the development is almost exclusively concerned with the first subject, which is worked out with the utmost ingenuity and effectiveness. Early in the development section Schumann introduces the triangle, and in one place actually gives it the theme. This use of it caused a musical scandal in 1842, for the triangle, up to that time, had not appeared in serious orchestral writing. (Today, with tom-toms and wind-machines grown commonplace, it seems old-fashioned.) Toward the end of the movement, a third theme is heard, chiefly sung, like the second, by clarinets and bassoons. But it is, as it were, an afterthought, and soon after it appears the movement comes to a brilliant close. The slow movement is a lovely song, at first for the violins, and then, after a moment in the wood-wind, for the 'cellos. Toward the end it goes back to the wood-wind. One theme suffices for the whole; the second is no more than an

echo of the first. Fragments from the two are woven into an
exquisite fabric in the middle, but there is no real development, and the whole thing, first and last, is no more than a
song with orchestral accompaniment. In this respect it
suggests the last movement of Schubert's Unfinished Symphony, another example of unsurpassable beauty wedded
to the starkest simplicity of design. As Philip H. Goepp
says, "the larghetto is one simple, sincere song, a stay of
merriment; but there is no sadness, rather a settled, deep
content." One lies under the trees and listens to the birds.
In the *Gasthaus* down under the hill there is a pretty
Biermad'l. It is May Day.

The scherzo starts off in D minor, but its abounding ani-
mal spirits offer one more proof that the common superstition about the melancholy of the minor keys is a superstition and no more. It has two trios and a number of
delightful changes in time and tempo, and ends with a
drum-roll in D major and a whisper in the reeds. Then the
whole orchestra plunges into the finale, an uproarious dance
with moments of pause and reflection. Two separate dance
themes, both of them extremely boisterous, stand in contrast to the main subject, and that subject itself is so considerably modified that it takes on the aspect of a fourth
theme. Faint echoes of the trumpet call of the first movement are heard; the piping grows fast and furious; it all
ends with a loud clatter. Schumann's finales are always
lively, but he never wrote a livelier. It has all the rhythmic
rattle of a barn dance; it almost suggests the celebrated hoedown finale of Dvořák's "From the New World." One need

know nothing whatsoever of music to respond to so deft a tickling of the midriff. Unlike many other great composers Schumann was not an infant prodigy. Again unlike the majority, he was a man of easy means and seldom had to work for money. Yet again, he differed from most in being a university graduate and a man of wide and sound culture. His father was a well-to-do publisher, and he himself was designed for the law, and pursued the study of that laborious science at the Universities of Leipzig and Heidelberg. His parents were not musicians, and though they had him instructed in music in his childhood, as is almost the universal custom in Germany, they opposed his adoption of a musical career, and it is probable that if his father had lived he would have ended as a lawyer. But his father died when he was 16, and he found his mother, though firmly opposed to his plans, a good deal easier to wheedle. It was not, however, until after four years of that wheedling that he finally induced her to let him abandon his Institutes. She then put the decision into the hands of Friedrich Wieck of Leipzig, who not only made of the young Saxon one of the greatest musicians of all time, but also (though unwillingly) provided him with the best wife that a great musician ever had.

This wife was Wieck's daughter, Clara. When Schumann entered the Wieck household, in 1830, Clara was a child of 11 years, and for four or five years thereafter he regarded her as a little sister. In 1834, indeed, we find him betrothed to a certain Countess Ernestine von Fricken, another pupil of Wieck's, and writing to Clara about it. But it was not long before he found that it was not the Countess that he loved but little Clara, and after the summer of 1835 his wooing of her went on undisguised. Clara was willing, but Papa Wieck refused to countenance the match, not only because she was very young, but also and chiefly because he was unaccountably suspicious of Schumann.

The latter, determined to have his way, appealed to the Leipzig courts for permission to marry Clara without her father's consent, but the case dragged on for month after month without a decision being reached, and in the end the lovers waited until the day Clara was 21 years old. Schumann was then 30.

No happier marriage is recorded in human history. Clara was not only a beautiful and extremely good tempered girl, but also one of the greatest pianists of her time, and the rest of her long life—she lived to be 77 and survived her husband by 40 years—was devoted chiefly to playing his music. No one, it is probable, has ever played it better, and surely no one has ever played it with greater devotion. She was the founder of the Schumann cult, not only in Germany but also in France, England and Russia, and in her old age she was regarded with almost superstitious veneration by the growing circle of Schumann disciples. Johannes Brahms looked upon her almost as a mother, as he had looked upon Schumann as a father, and when she could play no longer and poverty pressed upon her, he insisted upon making her an allowance of 10,000 marks a year. Her death was a staggering blow to Brahms, and he survived her by scarcely a year.

Brahms' devotion was not merely sentimental; he owed

well nigh everything to the Schumann's paper, the *Neue Zeitschrift für Musik*, that made a celebrity of him, and he was welcomed as a son in the Schumann home. The elder composer was always alert for fresh talent, and his influence upon the development of music in his time was due even more to his critical penetration and enthusiasm than to his actual compositions. So long as he wrote for it, the *Zeitschrift* remained the foremost musical authority of Germany, and hence of the world. He not only wrote with sound understanding, but also with uncommon grace and charm, and some of his articles hold a secure place among the classics of criticism. Many of them were cast in the form of discussions among the members of a mythical brotherhood of musicians called the Davidsbund, the chiefs of which were Florestan and Eusebius, and Schumann sometimes used one or another of these names in signing his articles. The Florestan Club [5] of Baltimore got its name from Schumann's Florestan.

The composer was a man of rugged frame and distinguished appearance, but there was a neurotic element in him which early showed itself, and in the end he suffered a derangement in mind. On February 27, 1854, in a fit of melancholy, he left his home at Düsseldorf and threw himself into the Rhine. He was recognized and taken home, but at his own request he was soon afterward removed to a pri-

[5] "Florestan" is the happy hero in Schumann's piano composition, "Davidsbundler." The club was comprised of leading professional and amateur music lovers. Among the members were several from the Saturday Night Club, including Mencken. The club lasted about six years.

vate insane asylum near Bonn. In 1855 he improved greatly and was able to write letters and to receive visits from his friends, but he never recovered sufficiently to resume composition. He died on July 29, 1856, in the arms of his faithful wife. She survived until May 20, 1896.

Schumann's fame, while he lived, was greatly overshadowed by the much more showy celebrity of Mendelssohn. He himself helped to establish this false valuation by his extremely generous praise of his great rival. Outside of Germany, in particular, he was underestimated for a long while. But during the last 40 years he has come into his own, and today he ranks among the undisputed masters of the tonal art, with only such colossi as Bach, Beethoven and Mozart clearly above him. So greatly has the estimation of him grown, indeed, that, by a sort of reaction, the talents of Mendelssohn have come to be pooh-poohed. Schumann, if he were alive, would be taking measures against too ardent transvaluation. No one understood Mendelssohn better than he did, and no one could more clearly discern the very real genius behind the superficial elegance of the fashionable composer. Schumann, you may be sure, would not be forgetting that it was Mendelssohn who resurrected Bach, and made the world acknowledge his imperial dignity.

❖❖❖❖❖❖❖❖❖❖❖

Mendelssohn

(1 8 0 9 – 4 7)

From the Baltimore *Evening Sun*, 1910.

ON THE HUNDRED and first birthday of Felix Mendelssohn-Bartholdy, who was born at Hamburg February 3, 1809, the world finds itself rather painfully undecided as to his true rank in music. While he lived there was no such uncertainty, for London and Leipzig, and even Paris and Vienna, joined in hailing him as the first musical gentleman of Europe. No other composer or conductor ever enjoyed such extravagant adulation. He was the acknowledged emperor of the baton; his pilgrimages from city to city were triumphal progresses: every new composition from his facile pen reduced the world to stupefied amazement and admiration.

Naturally enough, that sort of worship could not last. When Mendelssohn died, at the age of 38, there were already mad mullahs who preached a holy war against him, and soon afterward they began to make multitudes of converts. According to one critic, the whole history of music since then has been a history of Mendelssohn's decline and Schumann's rise. Today there is a wide disposition to dismiss the greatest of Gewandhaus stars with a patronizing smile, as an elegant young man who had creditable ideals and did his best, but never got very far. His "Elijah", we are told, is headed toward the massed choirs of Youngstown and

Kalamazoo; his "Midsummer Night's Dream" music has a saccharine smack and his Italian symphony, heard after the inflammatory tone-poems of the moment, induce a fitful and uncomfortable slumber.

So, at least, say the judges who sit solemnly in the musical sanhedrim, and it may be admitted without hesitation that many of the counts in their indictment are well founded. No one would dream today of comparing the Scotch Symphony to the Third and Fifth of Beethoven, nor even to the Second, and yet that very thing was done by the exuberant Leipzigers in the month of March, 1842, when its banal strophes first fell upon their ears. In the same way the "Midsummer Night's Dream" music has long ceased to lift audiences to their feet, and it is becoming more and more difficult for piano players to get money for performing his fantasias and variations. Beside our latter-day tone-masters and the giants of all time Mendelssohn seems puny enough. One finds no truly moving content in his music: it touches the deeper emotions but seldom: more often it is merely pretty.

But who shall deny the charm of that prettiness? Where, in all music, do musical phrases lead us so delightfully to fairyland as in Mendelssohn's score for Shakespeare's immortal fantasy? What other composer has ever entered, with so much feeling and understanding, into the great Elizabethan's romantic mood? But Aristophanes, of course, was not Euripides, and so it is not surprising that when Mendelssohn tackled tragedy the effect was that of Corot painting a battlepiece. Like all young men of the thirties, he was a romanticist, but he was too civilized to yield to gusty emotions. A man, to do that, must be something of a barbarian, as Beethoven was, and Bach and Wagner. Mendelssohn was no barbarian.

And yet, as we have observed, the world must grant him splendid gifts. His talent always trembled upon the brink of genius. In his Violin Concerto, in some of his quartets, in "Elijah", and even in his piano music, there are purple moments which suggest the notion that a true poet may have lurked beneath the fashionable exterior. Mendelssohn died at 38, at which age Beethoven was just coming to artistic maturity. What he might have given to us had he lived through another generation is beyond all prophecy, but we may well speak of the things he did give us with profound respect. If it is true, as the learned tell us, that he missed real greatness, it is certainly no less true that he missed it by no more than a hairbreadth.

◇◇◇◇◇◇◇◇◇◇◇

Dvořák

(1841–1904)

AN AMERICAN SYMPHONY

From the Baltimore *Evening Sun*, October 19, 1916.

ANTONIN DVOŘÁK's symphony, "Z nového světa" (From the New World) which Mr. Strube and his estimable tone-artists are to unroll at the Lyric on Friday evening, was written in 1894 or thereabouts, while old Antonin was undergoing three years' penal servitude in New York. He had come to America in 1892 to become director of a conservatory, and, like many other visiting musicians (for example, Paderewski) he had been greatly intrigued by the lively niggerish swing of American popular music. The result was that he gave a lot of hard study to American folk-song, and particularly to the folk-song of the Negroes, and the second result was a group of three very excellent compositions—his string quartet in F, his string quintet in E flat and the aforesaid "From the New World."

The latter made an immediate success and has since remained one of the most popular works in the classical repertoire. A fashion of sniffling at it has grown up among the musical pundits, but the fact is not of much significance, for exactly the same sniffs are directed at a number of indubitable masterpieces, including Beethoven's incomparable Eighth Symphony, which Mr. Strube presented last season. The truth is that "From the New World" is a first-rate work of art, honestly constructed and superbly written. It is clear; it is ingenious; it is sound; it is beautiful. If, made mellow by its luscious phrases, you find yourself rolling your eyes at the performance, then please, I prithee, do not blush. It is well worth an oscillation or two of even the most cultured eye. You will search a long while, indeed, among the symphonies of these later years before you find better writing and better music.

The question as to how much of the work is Bohemian

and how much American has long engaged those who delight in musical anatomizing, and the weight of opinion seems to be that the composer's nationality over-balanced his purpose, which was to introduce Americans to their own music. The verdict is both platitudinous and unsound. It is platitudinous because all art is revealed in terms of the artist's temperament, and in Dvořák's case temperament was indistinguishable from nationality. He was, indeed a Bohemian of the Bohemians, and he could no more conceal the fact when he sat down to write music than he could change the contours of his peculiarly baroque and dog-like visage. And it is unsound because even the most cursory examination shows enough genuine niggerishness in his symphony to outfit a Kerry Mills. He was not trying, remember, to write a suite in ragtime; he was trying to write a symphony—a thing rigid in its design and even in its details. The form he worked in was German and the temperament he brought to the business was Bohemian, but the materials he made use of were at least two-thirds American, and so he was quite right in calling the product an American symphony.

If you don't believe it get a good edition of the Jubilee Songs and the score of the symphony and go through them at the piano on some quiet Sunday afternoon. In the very first subject of the first movement you will find a plain reminiscence of "Roll, Jordan, Roll", and in the characteristic jumpy figure which immediately follows (and which holds together the whole first movement) you will encounter an old friend. This figure, perhaps, cannot be traced to any definite Negro song or dance, but it is nevertheless as indubitably niggerish as hog and hominy. And out of it (first tooted by the woodwind, and then taken up by the strings) there grows a subject which strangely suggests "Didn't My Lord Deliver Daniel?", and on top of it there comes a palpable borrowing from "Oh, Redeemed", unchanged even in key. These three subjects, beautifully worked out, supply the materials of the whole first movement. Nothing else is in it. And all three come straight from the Jubilee Songs.

The other movements show fewer direct borrowings. They are, indeed, rather paraphrases of American music than direct imitations of it. Dvořák, one fancies, was inspired to undertake the work by the powerful appeal of one or two tunes, especially "Roll, Jordan, Roll"—and exhausted them in his first movement. But in the second movement—the succulent and famous largo—there is still a clear echo from the plantation. The curve of the melody is his own, but the rhythm owes much to such songs as "Nobody Knows the Trouble I See", and "Rise, Mourners", and the plaintive, wailing spirit of Negro music is in every measure of it. Turn to "Many Thousands Gone", so beautifully realized in later years by S. Coleridge-Taylor, and you will note the kinship at once. Even in the wild episode which breaks into the lament there is true Negro color. No Negro, it may be admitted, ever danced to this precise tune, but many a Negro has shaken his legs to tunes curiously like it.

The scherzo goes further afield. One discerns in it many characteristic fragments of Negro rhythm, but melodically it is sophisticated and European. Its two surpassingly beautiful episodes are wholly beyond the range of Negro song; they suggest Schubert, not Booker Washington. Moreover, the very time signature is exotic, for the blackamoor almost invariably hoofs his fandangos and sets up his caterwauling in four-four time; the triple measure belongs to the late stage of musical evolution. But in the last movement—a very fine piece of writing—Dvořák returns to his muttons. Here, as in the largo, it is difficult to track down definite sources, but here again the swing and color are unmistakably niggerish. The thing starts off with a loud braying and stamping of feet; it proceeds to a wild hoedown; it ends in whoops and snorts that die down to whispers. For all its prodigality of melody, a Negro-like monotony is in it; the violas drone a fierce and savage figure while woodwind and fiddles sport with fragments from the second and third movements above them. And toward the end, against a musical fabric made up of these figures and others, all the choirs in their turn fling a barbarous syncopated phrase that infallibly suggests the loud cries of a Negro dance.

The last movement, it is true, contains some of the best writing that Dvořák ever did. It is, for him, extremely complex in structure; there is scarcely a moment of pure homophony, the polyphonic web is elaborately woven. And yet, for all that intricacy of design, there is perfect clarity in it, and even a sort of naked simplicity. One feels that he has gone beyond the plantation songs to the rude and violent chants of the jungle; the atmosphere is one of frank savagery; it is difficult to listen to the rush of sound without being stirred.

But the first movement, after all, is the most remarkable of the four, for in it Dvořák accomplishes something that he seldom accomplished elsewhere. That is to say, he sticks to the strict sonata form, without episodes, and is almost as austere in his use of materials as Brahms. The old fellow was not at ease in this sort of writing. His natural bent was toward a gigantic and somewhat disorderly piling up of ideas, as in his Dumky trio, his string quartets and the scherzo of the present symphony. So many melodies buzzed in his head that it was hard for him to settle down to the laborious development of two or three; new ones were always pressing to be heard. But here, as I say, he retained his Bohemian exuberance with German *Zucht*, and the result is a very fine piece of writing, indeed.

On the side of instrumentation the whole symphony is extremely lovely. Dvořák's long years of service in the orchestra pit gave him a firm grip upon all the tricks, and so his score glows with gorgeous colors. Give your ear to the largo if you would hear a perfect concord of sounds. From the incomparable opening chords to the last arpeggio of the muted violins there is one long procession of beauties. And in the last movement, again, he shows himself a genuine master of the orchestra. The thing often sounds barbarously harsh and naïf, but there is deft and thoughtful workmanship in every measure of it.

Dvořák was the son of a Bohemian tavern-keeper and butcher, and his father designed him for the latter art. But he took to playing the fiddle in his nonage and soon became so proficient that he decided to study music. This, however, was easier planned than done, for the elder Dvořák was poor and there were few competent teachers in the neighborhood. When he was 12 years old he was sent to a town called Zlonitz, where an uncle lived, and there he had some lessons from an organist named Leihmann. Regarding this Leihmann the chronicle is otherwise silent, but he seems to have taught young Antonin the rudiments of organ-playing and enough harmony to keep him going. His first composition belongs to this period. It was a polka for the village band at home. The polka itself seems to have been very creditable, but in scoring it the boy forgot to transpose the trumpet part, and so the first performance ended with yells for the police.

Late in his teens Dvořák went to Prague, and there, for a good many years, he played the fiddle in theater orchestras and made a scanty living teaching. All the while he was piling up compositions on his shelf—songs, string quartets, operettas, even a symphony or two. Most of these things were unperformed: there seemed little likelihood that he would ever be heard of beyond the town. He was 32 years old before he got his chance. It came when he was commissoned to write music for a cantata by Hálek, a favorite Bohemian poet. The result was "Die Erben des Weissen Berges" ("The Heirs of the White Mountains"). It made a considerable success, and some of Antonin's cobwebbed compositions were exhumed and performed, including a symphony in E flat never published. But this success led to little, and Dvořák remained unknown in the great world until he was discovered by Brahms in 1877. Brahms then did for him what Schumann, years before, had done for Brahms himself; that is, he advised him, encouraged him and, more important still, talked about him. A year later Dvořák published his "Slavische Tänze" and was a made man. These dances swept through Germany as Brahms' Hungarian dances had swept through it a few years before. The musical publishers, once so coy, now besieged the composer with offers, and he answered them with a flood of manuscripts. By 1880 he was securely on his legs.

Hans von Bülow, a sincere admirer of Dvořák, almost cooked his goose for him by calling him "Der Bauer im Frack" (the peasant in a dress-coat). This apt and yet unfortunate label has stuck to him ever since, and most criticism of his work has taken color from it. The result is that he is commonly regarded as a sort of inspired clodhopper, with a fine musical gift but with little genuine musical skill. Nothing could be further from the truth. The fact is that Dvořák, though almost self-taught, acquired a sound and sure command of the methods of composition, and that his best work is highly discreet and sophisticated. He had a better command of polyphony, indeed, than Schubert, but like Schubert he was often carried away by the exuberance of his own verbosity. Melodies gurgled from him like cider from a jug; he could scarcely get one to paper before another came bubbling out. The consequence, particularly in his early compositions, is a confusing oversupply of materials. They seem, at times, to be no more than disorderly strings of unrelated episodes.

But in his later years he made a deliberate effort to bring his genius into better discipline, and the effects of that effort are plainly to be seen in the New World symphony. The first movement, in particular, is full of evidence of a restraining intent. The three subjects, for all their barbaric color, are still somewhat terse and austere—that is, for Dvořák—and their working out is carried on with a relentlessness that he seldom shows anywhere else. No episodes creep in to relieve and corrupt the business; what other material is used (putting aside the monotonous, jiggling figure which runs from end to end) is manifestly derived from them; the whole thing hangs together; there is unbroken clarity in it.

In the largo the composer returns to easier devices. The form is that of a simple lyric, with a sharp and characteristic change of mood in the middle section. This is the sort of writing that came most gratefully to Dvořák's hand; one finds it again in the most familiar of all his compositions, the celebrated "Humoresque." And in the scherzo, as has been said, two episodes of extraordinary beauty are dragged in, almost by the heels. But in the gaudy and turbulent last movement, for all the piling up of tunes, there is a return to letter form, and toward the end of it the composer rises to brilliant heights. Here the whole symphony is rehearsed. Bits of the first and second movements are borrowed to adorn the fabric; there are violent contrasts in tempo, rhythm and dynamics; the thing goes with a rush that conceals its ingenuity of design and execution.

Dvořák had a hard time of it as a young man. His salary at Prague, where he was organist for a while, was $80 a year. But after success overtook him, toward middle life, he prospered financially as well as artistically, and during his three years in New York he received $15,000 a year, besides what he could make playing at weddings. A portrait of the period, printed in Grove's Dictionary of Music, shows him elegantly accoutered, with no less than three diamond horseshoes in his cravat. In 1891 he was given the degree of doctor of music by Cambridge University. He died on May 1, 1904.

OPERAS
AND OPERETTAS

⚘

Opera

From *The Allied Arts*, Prejudices: Second Series, 1920, pp. 197–200.
First printed in the New York *Evening Mail*, Feb. 22, 1918.
Included in A Mencken Chrestomathy, 1949, pp. 545–7.

Opera, to a person genuinely fond of aural beauty, must inevitably appear tawdry and obnoxious, if only because it presents aural beauty in a frame of purely visual gaudiness, with overtones of the grossest sexual provocation. It is chiefly supported in all countries by the same sort of wealthy sensualists who also support musical comedy. One finds in the directors' room the traditional stock company of the stage-door alley. Such vermin, of course, pose in the newspapers as devout and almost fanatical partisans of art. But one has merely to observe the sort of opera they think is good to get the measure of their actual artistic discrimination.

The genuine music-lover may accept the carnal husk of opera to get at the kernel of actual music within, but that is no sign that he approves the carnal husk or enjoys gnawing through it. Most musicians, indeed, prefer to hear operatic music outside the opera house; that is why one so often hears such lowly things, say, as "The Ride of the Valkyrie" in the concert hall. "The Ride of the Valkyrie" has a certain intrinsic value as pure music; played by a competent orchestra it may give civilized pleasure. But as it is commonly performed in an opera house, with a posse of fat beldames throwing themselves about the stage, it can only produce the effect of a dose of ipecacuanha. The sort of person who actually delights in such spectacles is the sort of person who delights in gas-pipe furniture. Such half-wits are in a majority in every opera house west of the Rhine. They go to the opera, not to hear music, not even to hear bad music, but merely to see a more or less obscene circus. A few, perhaps, have a further purpose; they desire to assist in that circus, to show themselves in the capacity of fashionables, to enchant the yokelry with their splendor. But the majority must be content with the more modest aim. What they get for the outrageous prices they pay for seats is a chance to feast their eyes upon glittering members of the superior *demi-monde*, and to abase their groveling souls before magnificoes on their own side of the footlights. They esteem a performance, not in proportion as true music is on tap, but in proportion as the display of notorious characters on the stage is copious, and the exhibition of wealth in the boxes is lavish. A soprano who can gargle her way up to F sharp *in alt* is more to such simple souls than a whole drove of Johann Sebastian Bachs; her one real rival in the entire domain of art is the contralto who has a pension from a former grand duke and is reported to be *enceinte* by several stockbrokers.

The music that such ignobles applaud is often quite as shoddy as they are themselves. To write a successful opera a knowledge of harmony and counterpoint is not enough; one must also be a sort of Barnum. All the first-rate musicians who have triumphed in the opera house have been skillful mountebanks as well. I need cite only Wagner and Richard Strauss. The business, indeed, has almost nothing to do with music. All the actual music one finds in many a popular opera—for example, "Thaïs"—mounts up to less than one may find in a pair of Gung'l waltzes. It is not this mild flavor of tone that fetches the crowd; it is the tinpot show that goes with it. An opera may have plenty of good music in it and fail, but if it has a good enough show it will succeed.

Such a composer as Wagner, of course, could not write even an opera without getting some music into it. In all of his works, even including "Parsifal", there are magnificent passages, and some of them are very long. Here his natural genius overcame him, and he forgot temporarily what it was about. But these magnificent passages pass unnoticed by the average opera audience. What it esteems in his music dramas is precisely what is cheapest and most mountebankish—for example, the more lascivious parts of "Tristan und Isolde." The sound music it dismisses as tedious. The Wagner it venerates is not the musician, but the showman. That he had a king for a backer and was seduced by Liszt's daughter—these facts, and not the fact of his stupendous talent, are the foundation stones of his fame in the opera house.

Greater men, lacking his touch of the quack, have failed where he succeeded—Beethoven, Schubert, Schumann, Brahms, Bach, Haydn. Not one of them produced a genuinely successful opera; most of them didn't even try. Imagine Brahms writing for the diamond horseshoe! Or Bach! Or Haydn! Beethoven attempted it, but made a mess of it; "Fidelio" survives today chiefly as a set of concert overtures. Schubert wrote more actual music every morning between 10 o'clock and lunch time than the average opera composer produces in 250 years, yet he always came a cropper in the opera house.

Grand Opera in English

From the Baltimore *Herald*, July 11, 1905.

Of all the theatrical or musical organizations that make annual visits to Baltimore, none is more heartily greeted and none more richly deserves public approval and support than the English Opera Company, managed by Col. Henry W. Savage. Organized a dozen years ago for the presentation of the better sort of light operas, it ran the gamut of Offenbach, Strauss and von Suppe. Then, struck by the fact that the American people liberally patronized German and French operettas sung in English, when these identical pieces, sung in German or French, were little encouraged, Colonel Savage came to the conclusion that the same thing would be true of the grand operas.

If we are not mistaken, the work he selected for his experiment was "Il Trovatore." Whatever was the opera, the result was a triumph, and since then the Savage company has sung nearly all the masterpieces of the world's great composers of dramatic music. Last year the repertoire included operas by Wagner, Verdi, Bizet, Puccini and Mascagni, and a second company, organized on the same principle, presented Wagner's religious music drama, "Parsifal." The latter organization attracted larger audiences than the Metropolitan Opera Company, despite its lack of celebrated stars, and the lesson of the season was that, given painstaking performances in English at reasonable prices, American audiences will cheerfully patronize grand opera.

There is no more reason why "Il Trovatore" should be sung in Italian [1] than there is that "Cyrano de Bergerac" should be played in French or "A Doll's House" in Norwegian. The libretto is not the important half of an opera, but it is comforting to be able to understand it. As Col. Savage's companies sing them, the books of such pieces as "Lohengrin" and "La Bohème" are easily comprehensible. That this fact adds infinitely to the enjoyment of the per-

---

[1] During the intervening 55 years since this article was written many of the foreign-language operas have been produced in English. However, it is still a controversial matter because the words, when translated into English do not fit the music as well as the words of the original language. Furthermore, there is almost inevitable distortion when words are sung, regardless of which language is set to tone.

formance is one recognized so many years ago that it is surprising that no other American manager ever thought of it. Joseph Addison, writing in the eighteenth number of the *Spectator*, on March 21, 1710, inveighed against the custom, then rapidly growing, of singing operas in Italian on the London stage.

"We no longer," he said, "understand the language of our stage; insomuch that I have often been afraid, when I have seen our Italian performers chattering in the vehemence of action, that they have been calling us names and abusing us among themselves. In the meantime I cannot forbear thinking how naturally an historian who writes two or three hundred years hence, and does not know the taste of his wise forefathers, will make the following reflection: 'In the beginning of the eighteenth century, the Italian tongue was so well understood in England that operas were acted on the public stage in that language!'"

And yet it took nearly two hundred years for a man to read the lesson in this protest and make a fortune by it. Let Colonel Savage roll up his millions! He deserves them.

The Tower Duet in *Il Trovatore*

Extracted from Mencken's review in the Baltimore *Herald*,
January 1, 1905.

. . . How WELL it was sung, and how simply!—even if Mr. Sheehan, who is a gentleman of no small heft, did seem to

stand in fear of falling from the window into the subcellar
of the tower. There was no platform in the tower and
Mr. Sheehan had to climb a ladder to reach the window. As
he arose he began—

> "Ah! how death still delayeth,
>   Lingers, or seems to fly,
> From him who longeth,
>   From him who longeth to die!"

Not until the second "longeth" did his curly black hair
appear above the sill of the barred window, and not until he
was near the end of "Farewell, love! Farewell, Leonora!
Farewell!" did he summon up courage to grip the bars and
lean out between them. His exit, too, was made painfully
and fearfully, and Leonora, singing plaintively below, was
plainly apprehensive lest he slip and come crashing down
upon her—200 pounds of healthy tenor, full of entrancing
melody. . . .

❖❖❖❖❖❖❖❖❖❖

The Mikado

From the Baltimore Evening Sun, November 29, 1910.

THE MEMORABLE first performance of this greatest of light
musical pieces was given on March 14, 1885, at the Savoy
Theater in London, the scene of all Gilbert and Sullivan
first nights for 15 years. "Pinafore" had gone before, and it
seemed impossible that the stupendous success of that de-

lightful piece should be repeated by the new one, but nevertheless the miracle was achieved. "The Mikado" took London by storm, and soon afterward it took the world by storm. Before the end of 1885 it was being played in Europe and America by fully 150 companies. One night, in October in this country alone, there were no less than 117 performances.

Some cities for awhile supported two, or even more, "Mikado" troupes. This was the case, for example, in Baltimore. The late John T. Ford bought the local rights to the piece from John Stetson and John A. McCaull, who had acquired the American rights from the author and composer, and it was planned that the piece should be given its first Baltimore performance at Ford's Opera House on the night of August 25, 1885, with George W. Denham, Pauline Harvey and other excellent old-timers in the cast. But meanwhile, a man named S. W. Fort, who was managing a small opera company at the Academy of Music, got hold of the score of the piece and proceeded to put it in rehearsal, rights or no rights. On August 17, a week before the announced date of the Ford opening, "The Mikado" was thus produced.

Mr. Ford at once proceeded to tackle Fort in the courts, but judicial processes, then as now, were exasperatingly slow, and it was a long while before the case was heard and disposed of. Meanwhile, the actual combat of company and company had come to a quicker and more satisfactory issue. That is to say, the Ford company, when it began business on August 25, at once took the shine from the efforts

PLATE VI · Saturday Night Club members and guests (November, 1913). Mencken is the first one, seated, in the lower left-hand corner. The others, in clockwise order around the table, are: Samuel Hamburger, Max Cathcart (standing), Paul Patterson, Frederick Colston (standing), Theodore Hemberger, Harry Bush, Willard Wright (standing), Frederick A. Kummer, Adelin Fermin, Dr. John Wade, Col. Joseph Wickes (a waiter, standing), Albert Hildebrandt, John Phelps, Max Brödel, Philip Green, Matthew Tinker, Folger McKinsey (with wing collar), David Bacharach, and Alexander H. McDannald

PLATE VII · Members of the Saturday Night Club and other guests at the 50th birthday party for Folger McKinsey, at his home on the Magothy River, August 29, 1916. From left to right: Folger McKinsey, Matthew Tinker, Dr. John Wade, Rev. D. Steffens * (in back, wearing a straw hat), Samuel Hamburger, Theodore Hemberger, Viktor Erpf * (with cane, wearing straw hat), Alexander H. McDannald, Albert Hildebrandt, Mencken, W. E. Moffett, Adolph Torovsky

* non-members

of the Fort company. Before long the only persons going to the Academy of Music to see "The Mikado" were those who could not squeeze their way into Ford's, which was packed from orchestra pit to frescoing at every performance. So Fort gave up the ghost.

Somewhat similar battles were fought out in all of the larger cities of the country. In those days the United States had no copyright treaty with England, and in consequence the rights of Gilbert and Sullivan had but little standing in our courts. American managers were not slow to take advantage of the fact. In the face of common justice and decency they produced the new opera, paying nothing for the privilege and relying upon the courts to stand by them. In New York the result was a bitter suit between Stetson and McCaull on the one side and Sydney Rosenfeld and H. C. Milner on the other.

Rosenfeld at that time was a dramatic hack in large practice, and it fell to his lot to "adapt" and enliven with native wit nine-tenths of the operettas imported (duty free) by the Broadway managers. It was in this manner that the libretto of "The Mikado" fell into his hands. Let it be said for him that whatever his failings otherwise, he had at least sense enough to see that it was impossible to improve upon Gilbert's humor. That is to say, he did little more than add a few stanzas to the topical songs; but the fact remained that he was a party to the pirating of the opera, and so Stetson and McCaull sued him for damages, and he was haled before a serpent of wisdom called Divver, I.

Divver was an Ulster man, and a foe to all foes of the

Irish. Therefore, when he heard that a man with the suspiciously Asiatic appellation of Rosenfeld was accused of making off with the goods of a man bearing the glorious old Gaelic name of Sullivan, he began to work his eyebrows menacingly and to bombard Rosenfeld with searching questions. On the Sullivan side, too, was the aforesaid McCaull, alas, who threw away these advantages. First of all, he admitted on the stand that he was a Kentuckian by birth and had never been in Ireland; secondly, he made a number of laughable mistakes in Irish geography; and thirdly, he let loose the awful secret that Sullivan was not an Irishman at all, but a loyal Englishman.

Rosenfeld won. The decision of the court was to the effect that there was no remedy at law for offenses committed against Englishmen by free American citizens. Whether or not Gilbert and Sullivan had really written "The Mikado" as claimed in their bill of complaint, was beside the point. The important thing was that they were foreigners who sought to set up a hateful monopoly on American soil. The courts of certain other states took a different view of the matter, but in general the absence of a copyright treaty made it practically impossible for Gilbert and Sullivan to enforce their rights, and so piracy went on. Within a few months, as has been mentioned, there were no less than 117 "Mikado" companies on the road.

The people of the United States were "Mikado" crazy for a year or more, as they had been "Pinafore" crazy some time before. Things Japanese acquired an absurd vogue. Women carried Japanese fans and wore Japanese kimonos and dressed their hair in some approach to the Japanese manner. The mincing step of Yum-Yum appeared in the land; chop-suey, mistaken for a Japanese dish, became a naturalized victual; the Mikado's yearning to make the punishment fit the crime gave the common speech a new phrase; parlor wits repeated, with never-failing success, the lordly Pooh-Bah's remark about the "corroborative detail designed to lend verisimilitude to an otherwise bald and unconvincing narrative"; his other remark, about the ultimate globule of primordial protoplasm, engendered a public interest in biology and sent the common people to the pages of Darwin, then a mere heretic and the favorite butt of windy homiletes.

Altogether, "The Mikado" left a deep mark upon the United States. It aroused a liking for clean humor, for grammatical music, for good taste on the stage, which has never wholly died out, despite the rise of slapstick musical comedy, with its obscene jokes, its deafening cacophony and its displays of lingerie. The opportunity is here for another Sullivan. A new comic opera of "The Mikado's" quality would make a success so startling that the hits of "Florodora", "The Belle of New York" and other such flapdoodle would be forgotten.

◇◇◇◇◇◇◇◇◇◇

The Passing of Gilbert

(1836–1911)

From the Baltimore *Evening Sun*, May 30, 1911.

How THE COMMON American conception of the English, as a stodgy and humorless folk, could so long withstand the fact of the Gilbert and Sullivan operas must ever remain one of the mysteries of international misunderstanding. Here, indeed, was wit that Aristophanes might have fathered; here was humor that Rabelais might have been proud to own. And yet it was the work of a thorough and unmitigated Englishman—of William Schwenck Gilbert, to wit—a man born in the heart of London, and one who seldom passed, in all his 75 years, out of hearing of Bow Bells.

Gilbert died yesterday—perhaps 15 years too late. His career really ended in 1896, when he and Sir Arthur Sullivan wrote "The Grand Duke", their last joint work. They had quarreled before—and made up. Now they quarreled for good. Sullivan, searching about for a new partner, found that there was but one Gilbert. Basil Hood, Comyns Carr and Arthur Wing Pinero tried their hands and failed. And Gilbert himself, seeking a new Sullivan, learned that a new Sullivan was not be found. Edward German came nearest —but "The Emerald Isle" was still miles from "The Mikado."

The Gilbert and Sullivan partnership, in truth, was absolutely unique. One looks in vain for parallels. Beaumont and Fletcher, Meilhac and Halévy, the Goncourts—these come to mind, but differences at once appear. Sullivan, without Gilbert, seemed to lose the gift of melody, and Gilbert, without Sullivan was parted from that exquisite humor which made him, even above Mark Twain, the merrymaker of his generation. The two men, working together for 15 years, found it impossible, after their separation, to work alone. Sullivan, cast adrift, took to the writing of oratorios and presently died. Gilbert settled down as a London magistrate and convulsed the world no longer.

The great quality of Gilbert's humor was its undying freshness, an apparent spontaneity which familiarity could not stale . . . "The Mikado" was given in Baltimore last year without the change of a line. Not one of Gilbert's jests of 1885 was omitted; not a single "local hit" was inserted to help out the comedians. And yet, after a quarter of a century, how delightfully brisk and breezy it seemed! How the crowds laughed once more at Pooh Bah's grotesque speeches and at the Mikado's incomparable song! And how Sullivan's tripping music tickled the ear!

The world will be a long while forgetting Gilbert and Sullivan. Every spring their great works will be revived. At this very moment "Pinafore", now 23 years old, is under way in New York. They made enormous contributions to the pleasure of the race. They left the world merrier than they found it. They were men whose lives were rich with honest striving and high achievement and useful service.

◇◇◇◇◇◇◇◇◇◇◇◇

Pinafore at 33

From the Baltimore *Evening Sun*, 1911.

"PINAFORE" made a hit in New York the other night—for the twentieth or thirtieth time in 33 years. How well that tripping Sullivan music wears; how fresh those Gilbert jokes seem after a third of a century! The operettas of Johann Strauss II are as dead, in this country, as the parlor melodramas of Bronson-Howard and Augustin Daly; Milloecker and Lecocq are forgotten; even Offenbach's devilish tunes are heard no more. But once a year, at the very least, we have a grand revival of "Pinafore" or "The Mikado", with lesser revivals between, and almost always the manager who makes the venture gets his money back, and a few extra banknotes for his pains. "The Mikado" was here last winter —badly sung, but still drawing crowds. And the innumerable Aborn companies fall back upon it or upon "Pinafore" whenever "The Bohemian Girl" grows stale and folks tire of "Robin Hood."

"Pinafore" had its first performance on any stage at the Opera Comique in London, on May 25, 1878. It made an instantaneous and colossal success, but not until late in the following autumn did it reach the United States. The first American performance was at the Old Boston Museum, on November 25, 1878, with Marie Wainwright as Josephine and Saide Martinot as Hebe. During Christmas week the late John T. Ford presented the piece in Baltimore, with

Blanche Chapman as Josephine. At the start Baltimore viewed it coldly, but soon crowds went flocking to hear it, and by and by it became so amazingly popular that there was profitable patronage, in this one town, for two companies—and the whole United States for a hundred!

Before or since, the American stage has never seen another such success. "Florodora" was a hit in its day, and so was "The Merry Widow", and so was "The Belle of New York", but the hit of "Pinafore" was greater than all of these rolled together. The wheezes of the libretto passed into the common speech; the music was upon the air of the country from dawn to dawn. At one time, it is said, no fewer than 160 performances were given in one night—by pretentious companies of good singers, by companies of children, by troupes of amateurs. Every fourth church choir tried the game. Pinafore threatened to become a separate trade—a profession within a profession—like Uncle-Tomming. Scores of fair warblers, later to delight us in other roles, made their bows as Josephine; scores of actors, male, not forgetting Richard Mansfield, got their starts as Dick Deadeye.

After a while, of course, the craze died down. "The Pirates of Penzance" and "Patience" followed quickly, with "Iolanthe." After them, in 1885, came "The Mikado", and another smashing hit. But "Pinafore", through all the years, has held the palm. No other comic opera ever written—no other stage play, indeed, of any sort—was ever so popular. "Uncle Tom's Cabin" may have more performances to its credit in the United States, but "Uncle Tom's Cabin" has never crossed the seas. "Pinafore", however, has been given, and with great success, wherever there are theaters—from Moscow to Buenos Aires, from Cape Town to Shanghai; in Madrid, Ottawa and Melbourne; even in Paris, Rome, Vienna and Berlin.

BAND MUSIC

Italian Bands

From the Baltimore *Evening Sun*, April 13, 1911.

IN MANY a perfumed, colytic barber shop, at this greening season, the head barber, when a hiatus appears in the procession of customers, retires to the ante-chamber behind the steam massaging engine and practices difficult trills and cadenzas upon the Bb clarinet or, perchance, upon the silver-plated baritone, or mayhap, upon the trombone or slip-horn. In brief, the summer park season dawns, and the dashing gentlemen of the Italian bands prepare for the fray. There is no work for Italian bands in winter, and so many of their members turn temporarily to the humbler arts—barbering, clothing cutting, poetry, boilermaking, politics or what not. But when the bock beer signs appear and the birds begin to chirp in the trees, then the call of harmony reaches them and their thoughts turn once again to the "William Tell" overture, the sextet from "Lucia di Lammermoor", the anvil chorus from "Il Trovatore" and all the other well-loved compositions of their repertoire.

No need to sing the praises of the Italian bands. We have all listened spell-bound to their spirited, blood-stirring music. Even when they play out of tune, with their trumpets screeching abominably and their *tempi* sadly obfuscated, there is yet a certain magic in their tunes. An Italian cornettist, or clarinetist or ophicleidist never loafs upon his job. He is at it, hammer and tongs, from the drop of the hat. He blows until his hair stands on end and his carotid arteries swell like soap bubbles and his ears grow a deep, effulgent crimson and his lungs seem about to fly to pieces. It is not work to him, but play; he loves music; he is having the time of his life. Frigid, indeed, is the hearer who can hearken unto such joyous blasts and not answer with sympathetic grunts.

The art of music in the United States owes a great debt to the hurricanic and romantic Italians. Before they began to fill the band stands of our summer parks the prevailing taste among us was for music of the cheapest and most trivial sort. Our native bands played ragtime endlessly, and they played it very badly. The marches of Sousa represented the Himalayan heights of their endeavor. Upon the huge repertoire of genuine band-music—dashing French marches, sonorous overtures, elaborate transcriptions of opera scenes —they turned their backs. The stuff they tackled came from Tinpan Alley, not from the Scala or the Champs de Mars, and even for Tinpan Alley it was dull.

Then came the invading Italians, their clarinets under their arms and enthusiasm in their hearts. I don't know the name of the first Italian band that appeared among us. There is, I believe, a difference of opinion over this matter among the Italian musicians themselves. But the first band to attract much attention, if I make no mistake, was one that set up its music-stands in the shell at Willow Grove Park, near Philadelphia, about 15 years ago. Such music as it made was a novelty to the plain people. Gilmore had toured the country, and Sousa had toured the country, and other professors of the brass had followed them—but at $1.50 a seat. Here was a band that played for nothing in a huge summer park, where anyone able to pay a few cents car fare was welcome to listen all he cared.

The result was a palpable hit—an enormous popular success. I once saw a crowd of 15,000 at Willow Grove, packed close about the shell and listening to this excellent band. It played, not silly ragtime, but honest music. The sextet from "Lucia", performed by two trumpets, two trombones, a baritone and a tenor, was its *pièce de résistance*— and the sextet from "Lucia" is still the masterpiece of all true Italian bands. It played, too, the quartet from "Rigoletto", the overture to "William Tell", the pilgrims' chorus and march from "Tannhäuser", the soldiers' chorus from "Faust", the great march from "Aïda", the tower scene from "Il Trovatore" (as duet, as I recall it, for trumpet and trombone), the wedding music from "Lohengrin", elaborate arrangements of "Don Giovanni", "The Barber of Seville", "Traviata", "Carmen", "Cavalleria Rusticana" (then the favorite of the hour), "Stradella" and "Lucrecia Borgia." Going further, it tackled the familiar ballet suites, the time-honored overtures. And after a while it plunged boldly into Tschaikovski's "1812" and other such things of fuming and fury.

There was cheapness in more than one of these transcriptions. True music was often subordinated to the convenience and glorification of the solo performer; the unspeakable cornet was heard too much; things were played which, to the educated ear, brought more pain than soothing: the gentlemen of the baton, borrowing a trick from Sousa, ran to monkey-shines and posing. But the net effect of the band's playing, and of the playing of the countless other bands which followed it, was stimulating and educational. A public made familiar with Donizetti began to sense the banality of Kerry Mills, and from Donizetti to Verdi the step was easy, and from Verdi upward easier still. True musical appreciation began to appear in the land. The applause following the *Pilgerchor* began to be louder than the *banzais* following "A Georgia Campmeeting." And that was progress.

Just how many Italian bands are now making ready for the summer I don't know, but the number must be well above 200. Practically every American city of 50,000 or more inhabitants has a trolley park of the first class, and in every trolley park there is an Italian band. Baltimore, in summer, sometimes has three or four. They are missionaries of good music, for however sorry their limitations and however degraded the taste of the town in which they play, their striving is always upward. I have seen an Italian director weep tears of joy when a request came up for a "Parsifal" arrangement that he had made with his own hand. Night after night he had to play the chorus with real anvils and real sparks, but he had hope in his heart. He remembered the time when even the anvil chorus was caviare. He looked forward ecstatically to the time when its first notes would bring down upon him a shower of beer bottles and bad eggs.

Let no true friend of music scorn the Italian trumpeters and B♭ clarinetists! For all their parabolic mustachios, their tinsel epaulettes, their anvils, their posing, their Leonora sobbing and their waving of the Stars and Stripes, they are yet doing a good work in this slowly civilizing Republic.

◆◆◆◆◆◆◆◆◆◆

Wind Music

From the Baltimore *Evening Sun*, May 25, 1925.

HAVING BROUGHT the Philadelphia Orchestra up to undisputed first place in the concert-hall, the ever-energetic Leopold Stokowski now works off some of his surplus steam by organizing a brass band. So far it has given but two concerts, both in private, but soon or late, I daresay, it will be forced out into the open. My advice to the nobility and gentry is to book seats for the first public concert the instant they go on sale. For here is richness, indeed! Aided by a friendly bootlegger I heard the second private concert in Philadelphia last Sunday. It was the middle of the week before I was fit for my usual literary and spiritual exercises.

Brass bands, of course, are numerous, and many of them are good ones. But this is a brass band of an entirely new sort. Stokowski has neither tried to batter his audience into unconsciousness with mere noise, in the manner of the Italian conductors, nor endeavored to make his band an imitation orchestra, in the fashion of John Philip Sousa. Instead he has sought, within the natural limits of his medium, to augment its flexibility, its variety, its dignity— in brief, to convert it into a first-rate musical instrument. I can only report that the results he achieves are *kolossal.* Here, at last, is a brass band that can play Bach!

But where are players for such super-bands to be obtained? Apparently Stokowski found no difficulty in getting them together. He began with the brass and wood-wind performers of the Philadelphia Orchestra, and added a few string players who could also toot. Volunteers began to wander in from the lesser Philadelphia orchestras. Soon there was a band of a hundred men. More came in. At last Sunday's concert there were one hundred and forty performers—and all of them played divinely!

The concert began with a Sousa march (followed by two more as encores) and proceeded to "The Blue Danube" waltz, Schubert's familiar "Moment Musical" (for woodwind), and Sibelius' "Finlandia." That was the first part. The second part consisted of three Wagner numbers: the entrance of the gods into Walhalla from "Das Rheingold", Wotan's Farewell and the *Feuerzauber* from "Die Walküre", and the funeral march from "Götterdämmerung." Another intermission, and then the climax: the Bach Passacaglia, hitherto arranged by Stokowski for orchestra, and now heard, perhaps for the first time, for brass band.

All these things were scored for the band by the conductor himself. Even the Sousa marches showed some new touches. Sousa himself used to play them with the aid of double-basses and a huge battery of percussion instruments. Stokowski omitted the double-basses and reduced the percussion to its usual orchestra strength, with only one bass drum and one set of kettle drums. The effect was superb. All the familiar rattle was gone; instead there was a clear, bell-like lovely sonority—a magnificent swirl of pure sound. If Sousa was not in the house he missed something. His marches were played perfectly for the first time.

"The Blue Danube", it seemed to me, was relatively a failure. The Strauss waltzes all need the voluptuous whine of the strings; trumpets are too blatant and forthright for them, and the woodwind, unsupported, is too cold. Whatever the cause, the immortal "Donau" descended, more than once, to mere prettiness. Its divine beeriness was gone. Strangely enough, "Finlandia" lost almost as much. The first part, to be sure, was magnificent—and the band took it in rapid tempo with astounding ease and precision. But the second part, reduced to the bald woodwind, lacked pathos. Here, too, the sentimentality of the catgut was missing. In the Schubert piece the woodwind got its revenge. It had the floor alone—and it made such loveliness as these ears have not heard since January 16, 1920.

But all this was merely preliminary: the concert really began with the *Einzug* from "Das Rheingold." Here Stokowski achieved a double triumph: first with his scoring and then with his conducting. The familiar music leaped into new life at the first note: one presently began lamenting that Wagner had written it for orchestra, not for brass band. There was endless variety and endless charm in the tone-color. Exquisite combinations followed one another enchantingly. And always there was almost perfect playing. What a first trumpet! What a pair of flutes! And what a row of trombones up there against the back-wall!

The "Walküre" piece was somewhat less effective, probably because it was overlong. It was a very warm afternoon, and even Wagner loses his potency when bald heads begin to glitter. But in the *Feuerzauber* Stokowski offered some effects of the very first caliber—not imitation orchestra effects, but undisguised band effects, yet how delicate always, how charmingly appropriate to the music! The *pianissimo* of the band toward the end became almost fairy-like. It seemed incredible that that great gang of men could play with so soft and exquisite a touch. The audience sat as silent as the dead.

The *Trauermarsch* went off almost as well, but the "Rheingold" scene, I think, remained the bright, shining star of the Wagner section. Ah, that there had been a slice of "Tristan und Isolde", of "Die Meistersinger" or of "Parsifal"! Maybe they will come later. For one, I'd like to hear the band tackle the *Liebestod*. Would it be sacrilege to hand that incomparable elegy over to gentlemen in bright yellow uniforms, blowing tubas on a warm Sunday afternoon? Answer one: you have not heard the Philadelphia Band. Answer two: you have heard the thing done by fat sopranos, horribly encased in tallow and talc.

Bach ended the day—and Bach at his most lordly. Perhaps the heat was beginning to tell: perhaps the transplantation of Bach to the modern orchestra, done in this case by Stokowski himself, has had an evil effect. Whatever the cause, it seemed to me that the Passacaglia was somewhat muddy in the first part—that the threads of the polyphony ran together. The clear line of the fiddles was missing, and the even clearer line of the 'cellos. The clarinets were poor substitutes. This, obviously was against reason. Bach wrote mainly for the organ: his actual orchestra was a band of oboes and flutes far more than it was a band of strings. A brass band—that is, a Stokowski brass band—should get nearer to him than even a grand orchestra. I can only report that the Passacaglia languished until near the end. Then it rose magnificently and passed off with truly thrilling doings by the trumpets and trombones.

As I have said, Stokowski's conducting was quite as remarkable as the skill he showed at writing for his band. He had the advantage, of course, of starting off with highly competent performers. His first trumpet, name unknown to me, was a genuine virtuoso: he had the best trombones I have ever heard. Superb music, too, came from his French horns, from his flutes and from his lower woodwind, and his drummers and cymbal-beaters showed immense skill. But there must have been plenty of second-rate players in the band, especially among the clarinets. If they were there, then good conducting concealed them. The band played almost perfectly. There was not a grunt or a bray from end to end. . . .

TEMPO DI VALSE

From *The Allied Arts*, PREJUDICES: SECOND SERIES, 1920, pp. 204–6.
First printed in the *Smart Set*, September, 1919, p. 40.
Included in A MENCKEN CHRESTOMATHY, 1949, pp. 541–2.

THE WALTZ never quite goes out of fashion; it is always just around the corner; every now and then it returns with a bang. And to the sore harassment and corruption, I suspect, of chemical purity. The popular dances that come and go are too gross to be very dangerous to civilized human beings; they suggest drinking beer out of buckets; the most elemental good taste is proof enough against them. But the waltz! Ah, the waltz, indeed! It is sneaking, insidious, disarming, lovely. It does its work, not like a college-yell or an explosion in a munitions plant, but like the rustle of trees, the murmur of the illimitable sea, the sweet gurgle of a pretty girl. The jazz-band fetches only vulgarians, barbarians, idiots, pigs. But there is a mystical something in "Wiener Blut" or "Künstlerleben" that fetches even philosophers.

The waltz, in fact, is magnificently improper—the art of tone turned lubricious. I venture to say that the compositions of Johann Strauss have lured more fair young creatures to complaisance than all the movie actors and white slave scouts since the fall of the Western Empire. There is something about a waltz that is irresistible. Try it on the fattest and sedatest or even upon the thinnest and most acidulous of women, and she will be ready, in ten minutes, for a stealthy smack behind the door—nay, she will forthwith impart the embarrassing news that her husband misunderstands her, and drinks too much and is going to Cleveland, O., on business tomorrow.

WEDDING MUSIC

❦

New Wedding March Needed

From the Baltimore *Sun*, June 14, 1908.

A NEW WEDDING MARCH is sorely needed. The march from "Lohengrin" is as archaic as populism, and the Mendelssohn march is a doddering antique. Time was when this last composition, by reason of the harmonic handsprings of its first measure, fell upon the ear with a pleasant tickle. But now such felonious modulations are common, and first-year students at the Peabody master them before passing on to greater difficulties of the C major triad. . . .

A marriage ceremony without "Lohengrin" would be just as binding as those of today. The bridegroom would look just as silly, the bride would smile just as radiantly and the nascent mother-in-law, would find the same indescribable afflatus of relief. And a wedding without the Mendelssohn march would be legal and impressive, too. It might not be so noisy as the wedding of today, but it would be just as spectacular and just as regular.

We believe that the constant performance of these ancient and curdled compositions is due to the laziness of church organists. To your average church organist each succeeding wedding is about as interesting as a new chin to a busy barber. He is paid so much money to make music while the bridal party marches up and down the aisle of sighs, and being eager to annex this honorarium with the least possible expenditure of manual labor, nervous energy and intellectual effort, he scatters his fingers across the keyboard in the ruts that are deepest and familiar. The result is always a mechanical and heartrending performance of the wedding marches of MM. Wagner and Mendelssohn. . . .

We believe that the time is ripe for some miraculously industrious organist to give some other wedding march a start. A hundred and one likely compositions occur to us. There is, for instance, the beautiful wedding music by Grieg, and there is again the wedding march in "A Waltz Dream." A properly gloomy composition of the same sort is a feature of Rubenstein's opera "Nero", and another serves as the closing chorus of "The Mikado." Offenbach wrote more than 20 wedding marches and Victor Herbert has written seven. Any one of the 345 galops, polkas and schottishes of Johann Strauss might be changed into a passable wedding march by slowing its tempo and fitting it with a fanfare, a pedal point and a cadenza.

However, it is not well to put too much faith in the present race of organists. They are not reformers; they hate to practice, and in music, as a fine art, they take very little interest. . . .

◇◇◇◇◇◇◇◇◇◇◇

Enter the Church Organist

The Wedding, A Stage Direction, from A BOOK OF BURLESQUES, pp. 56–8,
Alfred A. Knopf. (Original publishers John Lane, New York, N.Y.)

. . . THE ORGANIST is a tall, thin man of melancholy,
uraemic aspect, wearing a black slouch hat with a wide brim
and a yellow overcoat that barely reaches to his knees. A
pupil, in his youth, of a man who had once studied (briefly
and irregularly) with Charles-Marie Widor, he acquired
thereby the artistic temperament, and with it a vast fond-
ness for malt liquor. His mood this morning is acidulous
and depressed, for he spent yesterday evening in a Pilsner
ausschank with two former members of the Boston Symphony Orchestra, and it was 3 a.m. before they finally
agreed that Johann Sebastian Bach, all things considered,
was a greater man than Beethoven, and so parted amicably.
Sourness is the precise sensation that wells within him. He
feels vinegary; his blood runs cold; he wishes he could im-
merse himself in bicarbonate of soda. But the call of his art
is more potent than the protest of his poisoned and quaking
liver, and so he manfully climbs the spiral stairway to his
organ-loft.

Once there, he takes off his hat and overcoat, stoops down
to blow the dust off the organ keys, throws the electrical
switch which sets the bellows going, and then proceeds to
take off his shoes. This done, he takes his seat, reaches for
the pedals with his stockinged feet, tries an experimental
32-foot CCC, and then wanders gently into a Bach toccata.

It is his limbering-up piece: he always plays it as a prelude to a wedding job. It thus goes very smoothly and even brilliantly, but when he comes to the end of it and tackles the ensuing fugue he is quickly in difficulties, and after four or five stumbling repetitions of the subject he hurriedly improvises a crude coda and has done. Peering down into the church to see if his flounderings have had an audience, he sees two old maids enter, the one very tall and thin and the other somewhat brisk and bunchy.

They constitute the vanguard of the nuptial throng, and as they proceed hesitatingly up the centre aisle, eager for good seats but afraid to go too far, the organist wipes his palms upon his trouser legs, squares his shoulders, and plunges into the programme that he has played at all weddings for fifteen years past. It begins with Mendelssohn's *Spring Song, pianissimo.* Then comes Rubenstein's *Melody in F,* with a touch of *forte* towards the close, and then Nevin's *Oh, That We Two Were Maying,* and then the Chopin *Waltz in A flat,* opus 69, No. 1, and then the *Spring Song* again, and then a free fantasia upon *The Rosary,* and then a Moszkowski mazurka, and then the Dvořák *Humoresque* (with its heart-rending cry in the middle), and then some vague and turbulent thing (apparently the *disjecta membra* of another fugue), and then Tchaikovsky's *Autumn,* and then Elgar's *Salut d'Amour,* and then the *Spring Song* a third time, and then an hurrah or two from the Hallelujah Chorus, and then Chopin again, and Nevin, and Elgar, and . . .

CATHOLIC
CHURCH MUSIC

ह

From the Baltimore *Herald*, September 30, 1905.

POPE PIUS' effort to restore the early Gregorian music to the services of the Roman Catholic Church is evidently meeting with very gratifying success. The complete attainment of his purpose, particularly in the United States, will take much time, and it is unlikely that the venerable Pontiff will live to see it, but already the effect of his pronunciamento of a year ago is plain. Circles for the study of Gregorian chants have been formed in nearly every large city in the country, and in a few churches the restoration has been achieved without the slightest opposition. That his holiness' aim is a good one is agreed by everyone who is competent to judge; that it will be attained is sincerely to be hoped.

The battle against decadent church music is no new one in the Catholic Church. The Council of Trent, in 1561 wrestled with the problem. The widening knowledge of music at that time had led to the rise of a horde of composers, and most of them were hard at work writing masses for the church. Some of these masses, if we are to believe the ancient chroniclers, were fearfully and wonderfully made. One melody, the famous "L'Homme Armé" which the Crusaders are said to have sung before the walls of Jerusalem, appealed to a great many of the contemporary Gounods and Bachs, and they rang the changes upon it *ad nauseum*. Pope Pius IV, in disgust, laid the matter before the council, and at its suggestion appointed a board of eight cardinals to devise a remedy.

It is believed that a majority of this board favored the absolute prohibition of all music but the ancient plain song, but Cardinal Borromeo, the president, did not think this plan wise, and in the end his view prevailed. He admitted, however, the utter worthlessness of most of the church music of the day, and after a long discussion it was resolved to invite Giovanni Pierluigi da Palestrina, director of the music at St. John of Lateran, in Rome, to essay a mass which should avoid the defects of those then in use. Palestrina, instead of one, submitted three masses. The first and second were heard with approval, but the third far surpassed them. It is related that when the cardinals heard it they wept with delight, and that it was at once sung before the Pope in the Sistine chapel. Palestrina called it "Missa Papae Marcelli", and it still holds it place today as one of the most sublime compositions of all time.

Nevertheless, Palestrina's aid was merely temporary, and before long trashy music began to appear once more in the church services. At one time, in truth, the composers of masses borrowed melodic ideas from popular secular songs, much after the manner of the Salvation Army. Three years ago, in Italy, there occurred something almost as grotesque, the singing of a whole act of "Il Trovatore" as part of a church service. But now, thanks to Pope Pius, there will be an end to this incongruous mingling of the sacred and the profane. Unless the plans go for naught, church music will soon take its ancient, dignified place above and apart from all other music.

NATIONAL MUSIC

English Songs

From the Baltimore *Sun*, 1909.

THE GREAT CROWDS which attend the recurring national *saengerfests* show how firmly the German folk-song has established itself in the affections of the American people. It is not Germans only who go to the *saengerfests* as listeners, and it is not only Germans who take an active part in them. One of the best choruses in the *Saengerbund*, we are informed, is made up of Welsh coal miners living in Pennsylvania. In order that they may sing the beautiful German songs these men have tediously mastered the difficult German language. There are Irishmen in some of the choruses, too, and in nearly all of them there are Americans whose connection with the German soil is very remote.

All of this indicates how much may be accomplished in music by persistent endeavor. The Germans love their national music, and by devoting their leisure to singing it they have made all other races love it, too. The same thing, we believe, might be done for the folk-music of any other nation. If the public had frequent opportunity, for example, to hear the ancient part songs of old England it would be awake to their surpassing beauty.

The English madrigals deserve to be rescued from their dusty library shelves. They reflect, for all their studied polyphony, that bubbling joy in life which marked Tudor England. Something of the Elizabethans' delight in spring sunshine and the open road is in them. Like Elizabethan lyric verse, they express the emotions of an efficient and optimistic race. Many of them, true enough, are extremely difficult for modern singers, but that fact only adds to their interest.

Toward the middle of the seventeenth century the madrigal began to decline in the face of the prevailing movement toward prettiness. By 1667 we find busy Mr. Pepys rejoicing in its passing. Pepys is what we moderns have come to call, with graphic justic, a low-brow. An oboe cadenza, on his own unblushing confession, moved him to crocodile tears, but "the manner of setting words and repeating them out of order, and that with a number of voices," made him sick. Pepys' voice, it would appear, was *vox populi*, for the madrigal retired to the libraries.

Then came the glee [1] one of the very few forms of musical composition native to British soil. The glee was far less complex than the madrigal. Like the German folk-song, it made scarcely any demand upon vocal technique. Anyone with a healthy glottis could help out at glee singing, and for

---

[1] Glee, in old English (*gliv* or *gleo*) meant "music." The glee is properly an unaccompanied vocal work for male voices, harmonic rather than contrapuntal, and not in a fixed form.

eighty years nearly everyone in England did so. The famous Madrigal Society, formed in 1741 to revive the madrigal, was soon singing glees, and in 1783 came the Glee Club. Glees were sung at every fair and merry-making. They were the delight of the philosopher and peasant alike. Herbert Spencer, as a youth, found his chief recreation in glee-singing, and so did Charles Dickens.

The rise of the music-hall song, in the 70's obliterated the glee, and today it is almost forgotten. But only intelligent effort is needed, we believe, to restore it to its old place. The American people, whose love for music, if untutored, is at least boundless, would hail it with joy. Here is an opportunity for our English-born choir masters. Let them turn aside, now and then, from their anthems and give us a taste of the beautiful music of their country. They have the voices at hand, and they should be able to find the time. Here in Baltimore, during the winter, there are concerts of German song, in public or private, almost every night. Why not one concert a month of English Song?

Russian Music

Review of *My Musical Life* by Nikolay Andreyevich Rimsky-Korsakoff, translated by Judah A. Joffe, with an introduction by Carl Van Vechten, (New York: Alfred A. Knopf; 1923). Appeared in *American Mercury*, January, 1924.

THIS IS the full story—meticulous, humorless, full of expository passion—of the Immortal Five: Balakireff, Cui,

Musorgski, Borodin and Rimsky-Korsakoff himself. The book is enormous, and details are piled on without the slightest regard for the reader's time and patience. One plows through exhaustive criticisms, often highly waspish, of concerts given fifty and sixty years ago; one attends to minute discussions of forgotten musical politics. Nevertheless, the general effect of the tome is surely not that of boredom. It somehow holds the attention as securely as Thayer's monumental "Beethoven" or the memoirs of William Hickey. And no wonder, for the world that good Nikolay Andreyevich describes is a world that must always appear charming and more than half fabulous to western eyes—a world in which unfathomable causes constantly produced unimaginable effects—a world of occult motives, exotic emotions and bizarre personalities—in brief, the old Russia that went down to tragic ruin in 1917. Read about it in the memoirs of the late Count Witte, and one feels oneself magically set down—still with one's shoes shined, still neatly shaved with a Gillette!—at the court of Charlemagne, William the Conqueror, Genghis Khan. Read about it in Rimsky-Korsakoff's book, and one gets glimpses of Bagdad, Samarkand and points East.

The whole story of the Five, in fact, belongs to the grotesque. Not one of them had more than the most superficial grasp of the complex and highly scientific art that they came so near to revolutionizing. Balakireff, the leader, was a mathematician turned religious mystic and musical iconoclast; he believed until middle age that writing a fugue was, in some incomprehensible manner, as discreditable an act as robbing a blind man. Cui was a military engineer who died a lieutenant general. Borodin was a chemist with a weakness for what is now called Service; he wasted half his life spoiling charming Russian girls by turning them into lady doctors. Musorgski was a Guards officer brought down by drink to a job in a railway freight-station. Rimsky-Korsakoff himself was a naval officer. All of them, he says were as ignorant of the elements of music, as so many union musicians. They didn't even know the names of the common chords. Of instrumentation they knew only what was in Berlioz's "Traité d'Instrumentation"—most of it archaic. When Rimsky-Korsakoff, on being appointed professor of composition in St. Petersburg Conservatory— a typically Russian idea!—bought a *Harmonielehre* and began to experiment with canons, his fellow revolutionists repudiated him, and to the end of his life Balakireff despised him.

Nevertheless, these astounding ignoramuses actually made very lovely music, and if some of it, such as Musorgski's "Boris Godunoff" had to be translated into playable terms afterward, it at least had enough fundamental merit to make the translation feasible. Musorgski, in fact, though he was the most ignorant of them all, probably wrote the best music of them all. Until delirium tremens put an end to him, he believed fondly that successive fourths were just as good as successive thirds, that modulations required no preparation, and that no such thing as a French horn with keys existed. More, he regarded all hints to the contrary as gross insults. Rimsky-Korsakoff, alone amongst

them, was genuinely hospitable to the orthodox enlightenment. He learned instrumentation by the primitive process
of buying all the orchestral and band instruments, and blowing into them to find out what sort of sounds they would
make. The German *Harmonielehre* filled him with suspicion
that Bach, after all, must have known something, and
after a while it became a certainty. He then sat down and
wrote fifty fugues in succession! Later he got tired of polyphony and devoted himself chiefly to instrumentation.
He became, next to Richard Strauss, the most skillful master of that inordinately difficult art in Europe. Incidentally,
he and his friends taught Debussy and Schoenberg how to
get rid of the diatonic scale, and so paved the way for all
the cacophony that now delights advanced musical thinkers.

A curious tale, unfolded by Rimsky-Korsakoff with the
greatest earnestness and even indignation. A clumsy writer,
he yet writes brilliantly on occasion—for example, about the
low-comedy household of the Borodins, with dinner at 11
p.m. and half a dozen strange guests always snoring on the
sofa. Is there a lesson in the chronicle, say for American
composers? I half suspect that there is. What ails these
worthy men and makes their music, in general, so dreary
is not that they are incompetent technicians, as is often
alleged, but that they are far too competent. They are, in
other words, so magnificently trained in the standard tricks,
both orthodox and heterodox, that they can no longer leap
and prance as true artists should. The stuff they write is
correct, respectable, highly learned—but most of it remains
Kapellmeistermusik, nay, only too often mere *Augenmusik*.

PLATE VIII · Music session of the Saturday Night Club, April, 1937, second floor of St. Paul Street address. From left to right: Back row: W. E. Moffett, double bass; Frank C. Purdum, flute; Dr. Raymond Pearl, French horn; Adolph Torovsky, 'cello; H. E. Buchholz, librarian. Front row: Dr. Franklin Hazlehurst, violin; Louis Cheslock, violin; Israel Dorman, viola; Max Brödel, piano; Mencken, piano

PLATE IX · *Saturday Night Club room at Schell-huse's restaurant on Howard Street, April, 1937. Read-ing left to right: H. E. Buchholz, Dr. Raymond Pearl, W. E. Moffett, Max Brödel, Adolph Torovsky, Frank* C. Purdum, Israel Dorman, Mencken, Dr. Franklin Hazlehurst, Louis Cheslock (*waitresses, Miss Emma, Miss Helen*)

Let them give hard study to this history of the five untutored Slavs who wrote full-length symphonies without
ever having heard, as Rimsky-Korsakoff says, that the
seventh tends to progress downward.[2] Let them throw away
their harmony-books, loose their collars, and proceed to
write music.

[2] The chord seventh normally progresses downward—the scale
seventh (leading tone) generally resolves up.

POPULAR SONGS
OF THE PLAIN PEOPLE

❦

A Plea for the Old Songs

From the Baltimore *Sun*, 1909.

WHEN THE gamboling Lambs appeared at Ford's Opera House not long ago one of their number stepped out from the minstrel half-circle and, lifting up a bleating tenor voice warbled "Sweet Genevieve." The singer sang badly, even for a tenor, and the choristers who joined him in the refrain sang still worse, but all the same his song was rewarded with more applause than any other number brought forth during the entire evening. There were youngsters in that huge audience who then heard "Sweet Genevieve" for the first time, and there were oldsters beside them, perhaps, who heard it for the 500th, with an interval of twenty years since the 499th. One and all, they were charmed by its homely sentiment, its exquisite melody and its rich, simple harmony. It was old-fashioned, but it was perfect.

There are scores of other old songs that deserve to be rescued from the musical mortuaries. One hears them, at rare times, when some gathering of bald heads grows

mushy—at a class reunion, maybe, or at the fag end of a
particularly liquorish banquet. The old boys howl like wild
animals and their harmonies recall the quartets of the
vaudeville shows, but they really enjoy their own cacophony,
and at the bottom of it you will always find more than one
song with a touch of true feeling in it. There is that ancient
of the ancients, "Juanita", for instance. Say that it is banal
and over-sweet and you will be within your rights as a critic.
But say that it has no charm—that, in the broad sense, it is
not beautiful—and you will be saying that you have no
ears.

What has become of "In the Gloaming"? Who sings it
today? Perhaps a few doddering "lifers" in the penitentiary,
immersed there since 1880. No one else. But is the charm
of "In the Gloaming" really dead? Not at all. The song
writers have been trying to go it one better for thirty years,
but they have not succeeded. It remains the one best song
to sing to your Angeline on a moonlight night. Your father,
no doubt, sang it to you when you squalled. It is at once a
love song and a lullaby. Its singing measures melt the heart,
improve the digestion and calm the mind. It is bathos, but
it soothes—as bathos always does.

And where is that dear old allurian, "Silver Threads
Among the Gold"? Do the song writers of today write songs
like that? Of course, they don't. They are more learned
than the old-timers and have progressed far beyond the
simple, ever-reliable chords of the tonic and dominant, but
they have made no progress in the invention of luscious
melodies. When they are at their happiest they are garbling

and "adapting" the ancient tunes. Thus, when we wept over "Wait Till the Sun Shines, Nellie", we were paying unconscious tribute to a far older song, "How can it Ever Be?"—the immigrant form, it may be observed, of a German tune of almost appalling antiquity.

The old songs had a certain unblushing sincerity about them that the songs of today seem to lack. "Love Me, and the World is Mine", for example, is too pretentious and strenuous to be convincing. In singing it the vocalist gets out of breath. No man, actually in love, ever wooed his inamorata with such studied magnificence. The phrases are rococo; they require the support of arduous piano thumping. The song drips with perspiration and midnight oil. One finds no such tortuous elaboration in "Wait Till the Clouds Roll By." Here the words of love are as simple as the words of Francis Bacon, and the music is as frankly sentimental as a waltz by Chopin. Such songs please the girls and make for happy homes. If they were sung today, instead of the artificial, anarchistic compositions of the ragtime kings, there would be fewer divorces, less scandals in the newspapers and less sorrow at the domestic hearth.

The Folk-Song

From the Baltimore *Sun*, 1909.

IT IS A PLEASURE to welcome Dr. Max Friedlaender to Baltimore. He is a German scholar of the highest type, and his brief course of lectures in McCoy Hall upon the history of music, with particular references to German song, is proving to be of great interest. No man has a better knowledge of folk song than he: his critical writings upon the ancient peasant and student songs of Germany are accepted as authoritative by all. And he is by no means a narrow special-ist, burrowing in this one field, for he has also written an excellent biography of Schubert, a sound chorus manual and other books upon music, and has edited the compositions of Weber, Beethoven, Schumann and other German masters. A student of the celebrated Manuel Garcia and of Philip Spitta, he is a singer as well as a historian, a music-lover as well as a critic.

Dr. Friedlaender, among other things, has done good service by insisting upon the folk element in all great music. Practically all composers of the first rank, indeed, have grounded their music firmly upon their native folk song. Among the Germans this is plainly evident, as well as among the assertively national Magyars and Slavs. Bee-thoven and Mozart made free use of the old German melodies and dance forms, and so did Weber and the song writers. Even in Wagner the national flavor is unmistakable. His ideas are expressed in essentially German idioms; he is a German in his music even before he is a musician.

The artificiality and banality which mark the bulk of American music today—here, of course, only serious music is meant—are due, in the main, to what may be called an absurd fear of nationalism. Our composers, in a word, are afraid to write as Americans. They try to write German music, using German ideas and the German idiom, and the result is inevitably an air of tedious and unsuccessful effort. Dr. Dvořák preached against this madness, but the fashion is still against him. To be accepted as learned, one must laugh at him. An American phrase is sufficient to damn a string quartet; a hint of the banjo in an orchestral composition is an unpardonable sacrilege.

And yet, if we are ever to produce music worth while, we must do as the Germans have done. We must see in our national tunes, not mere triviality, but the germs of good music. We must lift up our national idioms as the Germans and Slavs and Latins have lifted up theirs. We must realize that, however much they may disgust the pallid conservatory professor, the banjo and the hoedown are yet a part of our national musical consciousness, and that we cannot hope to make much progress until we take them into account. An American trying to write like a German is essentially an absurdity. But an American trying to write as an American might conceivably thrill the world and give it something new in an old art.

The scholastic answer to all this that, saving the plantation note, there is no national note in American music; that America has no folk song. This answer contents the pundits, but a brief inspection proves, at bottom, it is merely one more proof that a man may be learned in music and yet have no ears.

◇◇◇◇◇◇◇

American Folk-Song

Review of *The American Song-Bag*, by Carl Sandburg (New York: Harcourt, Brace and Co.; 1927). Appeared in *American Mercury*, January, 1924.

THE TITLE of this book is aptly chosen. Sandburg has emptied into its pages the lyrical loot of his wanderings about the United States, with his guitar under his arm. There are songs in endless variety, 280 of them in all, set down precisely as he heard them—often, alas, somewhat defectively, but always with a grand gusto for the simple sentimentalities of the folk. What other American has studied the folk more assiduously, or to better profit? His poems have the authentic flavor of the soil in them—they are unmistakably American as the folk-melodies of Friedrich Schiller are unmistakably German—and from the same mine he has dredged the rich materials of his "Rootabaga Stories" and his "Abraham Lincoln." In compiling this "Songbag" he had the aid of a huge array of collaborators, ranging from contrapuntists and professors of sociology to cowboys, Lake sailors, city loafers, and roistering students in far-flung "colleges" of the wheat country. But mainly the thing is his own. His running commentary on the songs is charming indeed. The volume would lose three-fourths of its peculiar interest if there were no Sandburg in it.

Now and then, to be sure, he nods: it would be astonishing, in so vast a collection, if he did not. Let him make note, in his next edition, that "Josie," on page 84, is simply a

mauled version of "Ain't Dat a Shame!", a famous vaudeville song of thirty years ago, now forgotten, and that the
"Boll Weevil Song", on page 8, borrows from the same
source. "Po' Boy", on page 30, is another decayed vaude-
villian of the palmy days, and "Common Bill", on page 62,
is a German folk-song, badly reported. The I. W. W. song,
"Hallelujah, I'm a Bum!", on page 184, was never written
by a wobbly, it is an ancient Salvation Army hymn, with
the tune unchanged. By the same token, "The Hearse Song"
on page 444, credited to the A. E. F., is the time-tattered
"Funeral March of a Marionette."

Some of the most familiar songs, it seems to me, are set
down inaccurately. In "Turkey in the Straw", for example,
the first two measures in the refrain should be repeated,
not in the series but successively. "Dese Bones Gwine to
Rise Again", on page 470, is a sad hash, both as to words
and as to music. Can it be that Sandburg has never heard
the one authentic, chemically pure first stanza:

> Some people say dat a nigger won't steal,
>> Dese bones shall rise again!
> But I caught one in my corn-fiel',
>> Dese bones shall rise again!

Also, what enemy of the aesthetic decencies gave him
"It's the Syme the Whole World Over" in $\frac{3}{4}$ time? [1] Cer-

---

[1] This song was one of the favorites of the Saturday Night Club.
It was sung in $\frac{3}{4}$ or $\frac{4}{4}$ time—according to how many seidels had
been downed!

tainly even the tots in the kindergartens must know by now that the tune is in common time—and that it is far more plaintive and lovely than the burlesque of it that Sandburg prints. Again, I must protest against the slaughter of "Lydia Pinkham" on page 210, and of "Hoosen Johnny", on page 164. Finally, I give notice that I did *not* write the accompaniment to "The Drunkard's Doom", on page 104, as a note politely says. But the whole book would be worth having if it contained only the priceless "I Got a Gal at the Head of the Holler", on page 320. Here, indeed, is American folk-song at its glorious best!

◇◇◇◇◇◇◇

The Music of the American Negro

From the Chicago Sunday *Tribune*, November 15, 1925.

THE FIRST BOOK of Negro songs ever published was brought out by the Rev. G. D. Pike of the American Missionary Association in 1873, and by 1892 its various editions had run to a total of 130,000 copies. But Pike was an uplifter, not a musician, and so his collection of the Negro spirituals, which were then called jubilee songs, was little more than a crude source book. All the bold and peculiar harmonies of the colored singer were lost. Pike had apparently intrusted the arrangement of his specimens to some manufacturers of Methodist hymns. Some of the best of them were thus converted into the sort of garbage that is heard at Billy Sunday [2] revivals.

[2] The famous barnstorming evangelist.

It was not until 1914, when the late Henry Edward Krehbiel, music critic of the New York Tribune, published his "Afro-American Folk Songs", that Negro song got any intelligent examination. Krehbiel was a German pedant of the dullest type (though he became a violent American patriot during the world war), but he at least had some knowledge of music, and so his study was a valuable one. Its defects lay in the incompleteness of his knowledge. He had to get nine-tenths of his songs at second hand, and not infrequently they reached him in a mutilated—or, worse still, in a clumsily embellished—state.

The gaps in his work are now admirably filled by James Weldon Johnson in "The Book of American Negro Spirituals." Mr. Johnson, himself a colored man, has gathered all his materials from original sources. He grew up in the south, he was interested in music from his earliest years, and with his brother, J. Rosamond Johnson, he was mainly responsible for the rise of what has since come to be known as jazz. But the Johnsons are by no means mere jazzhounds. On the contrary, they are both educated musicians. Thus their book is one of solid dignity and value. James Weldon Johnson discusses in a long preface the origin and nature of the spirituals, and J. Rosamond presents scores of them in his own arrangements.

BIRTH OF THE SPIRITUALS

The spirituals probably had a complex ancestry and are mulatto rather than Negro. All the original slaves brought in was a series of rhythms—many of them superb, but few of them accompanied by what Caucasians would recognize as melody. The Africans, to be sure, had tunes, but they were tunes of the vague, wandering sort that all other savages affect. They lacked what white musicians call form. There was no rhythm of structure under their rhythm of phrase, and so they could not convey that sense of design, that feeling of completion, which characterizes civilized melody.

But, as I say, the rhythms of the Negro were superb, and so all that was needed to make good songs was their reinforcement with melody. That melody, it is highly probable, came from the campmeeting, and at some time not earlier than the end of the eighteenth century. The whites in the south made no effort to educate their slaves in the arts, but they were greatly interested, after the first tours of Francis Wesley, in saving their souls, and that salvation was chiefly attempted, for obvious reasons, out of doors. There arose the campmeeting—and the campmeeting was a place of sturdy and even vociferous song. The Negroes memorized what they heard and then adapted it to their native rhythms. Thus the spirituals were born.

The purely Negro contribution to them—good rhythm—was the more important part, and by far. To this day Methodist hymns seem banal to musicians because they lack variety of rhythm; nine-tenths of them bang along in the same depressing sing-song. But the spirituals are full of rhythms of the utmost delicacy, and when they are sung properly—not by white frauds or by high toned dephlogisticated Negroes from Boston, but by black singers from the real south—they give immense pleasure to lovers of music.

Beethoven would have delighted in them, and Brahms, had he ever heard them, would have borrowed them for his uses—as, indeed, Dvořák did after him.

HARMONY PREFERRED TO MELODY

The Negroes, having started with Methodist hymns and improved them by joining them to decent rhythms, went a couple of steps farther. First, they improved them as mere melodies. That is, they displaced their obvious cadences with cadences of greater piquancy and relieved their monotony with bold modulations. Some of these modulations, as Mr. Krehbiel demonstrated in his book, went back to Africa. Savages knew nothing of the modes—or keys—that white men use. They see nothing wrong about inserting a glaring B flat or C sharp into the key of C major. They did this in many of the spirituals, and sometimes the effect was extraordinarily brilliant and thrilling.

Second, they improved the harmonies of the hymns, and for much the same reason. That is, they wandered into "errors" because they knew no better—and the errors turned out to be lush and lovely. The history of civilized music during the last two generations, indeed, has been largely a history of the discovery and adoption of such errors. When white musicians began to put them into music there were bitter protests from all the pedants, but now many of them have become quite orthodox, and music that is bare of them begins to seem bald and insipid. The Negroes were using some of them all the while. They were satisfactory to the African ear long before the Caucasian ear learned to tolerate them.

As Mr. Johnson shows the Negro is a harmonist far more than he is a melodist. He doesn't care much for tunes; the things that interest him are harmonies and rhythms. Let a crowd of colored fellows begin to sing any current song, however banal, and they will presently give it a new interest and dignity by introducing strange and often entrancing harmonies into it. They seem to have a natural talent for that sort of thing. A gang of white boys, attempting song together, will usually sing in unison, or stick to a few safe harmonies of the barber shop variety, but darkies almost always plunge out into deeper waters, and not infrequently, in the midst of harsh discords, they produce effects of extraordinary beauty.

DEBT TO AN UNKNOWN BARD

The spirituals are commonly called folk songs, and so the notion is abroad that they sprang full blown out of the folk—that they were written, not by individuals, but by whole groups. This is nonsense. In that sense, indeed, there is no such thing as a folk song. Folk songs are written, like all other songs, by individuals. All the folk have to do with them is to choose the ones that are to survive. Sometimes, true enough, repetition introduces changes into them, but those changes are not important. The basic song belongs to one bard, and to him alone.

Mr. Johnson tells of such a bard he knew as a boy in the

south, of the same surname as his own, but no relative—one "Singing" Johnson. Every southerner knows another. These minnesingers usually traveled about, singing for their keep. When they struck a new neighborhood they would make songs to fit what was going on in it—the advent of a new and powerful preacher, the conversion of a notorious sinner, a great flood or fire, the hanging of the local dare-devil. Most of these songs died in infancy, but a few always survived. The best of the survivors in the campmeeting category are the spirituals that every one knows today.

Ah, that we could discover the authors of some of them! What genius went to waste among the pre-confederate fundamentalists! But did it go to waste? Perhaps not. Only its possessors were lost. The black unknown who wrote "Swing Low, Sweet Chariot", "Deep River" and "Roll, Jordan, Roll"—for I suspect one bard wrote all three—left a heritage to his country that few white men have ever surpassed. He was one of the greatest poets we have ever produced, and he came so near to being our greatest musician that I hesitate to look for a match for him. There would be a monument to him in the south. He was worth a whole herd of Timrods.

MUSIC
AND OTHER VICES

※

Virtuous Vandalism

From the Baltimore *Evening Sun*, April 24, 1916.

A HEARING of Schumann's B flat symphony of late, otherwise a very soothing experience, was corrupted by the thought that music would be much the gainer if musicians could get over their superstitious reverence for the mere text of the musical classics. That reverence, indeed, is already subject to certain limitations; hands have been laid, at one time or another, upon most of the immortal oratorios, and even the awful name of Bach has not dissuaded certain German editors. But it still swathes the standard symphonies like some vast armor of rubber and angel food, and so imagination has to come to the aid of the flutes and fiddles when the band plays Schumann, Mozart, and even parts of Beethoven. One discerns, often quite clearly, what the reverend Master was aiming at, but just as often one fails to hear it in precise tones.

This is particularly true of Schumann, whose deficiency in instrumental cunning has passed into proverb. And in the B flat symphony, his first venture into the epic form, his failures are most numerous. More than once, obviously attempting to roll up tone into a moving climax, he succeeds only in muddling his colors. I remember one place—at the moment I can't recall where it is—where the strings and the brass storm at one another in furious figures. The blast of the brass, as the stage villains say, gets across—but the strings merely scream absurdly. The string passage suggests the bleating of sheep in the midst of a vast bellowing of bulls. Schumann overestimated the horsepower of fiddle music so far up the E string—or underestimated the full kick of the trumpets. . . . Other such soft spots are well known. Mr. Boyle's [1] highly sophisticated laying on of colors, brought into sharp contrast, was rather cruel to Schumann. He by no means offered better music, nor did he make the slightest pretension to any such herculean feat, but he undoubtedly offered a more skillful instrumentation.

Why, then, go on parroting *gaucheries* that Schumann himself, were he alive today, would have long since corrected? Why not call an ecumenical council, appoint a commission to see to such things, and then forget the sacrilege? As a self-elected delegate from heathendom, I nominate Dr. Richard Strauss as chairman. When all is said and done, Strauss probably knows more about writing for orchestra than any other two men that ever lived, not excluding

[1] On this same program the premiere of George Boyle's Piano Concerto was given.

Wagner. Surely no living rival, as Dr. Sunday would say, has anything on him. If, after hearing a new composition by Strauss, one turns to the music, one is invariably surprised to find how simple it is. The performance reveals so many purple moments, so staggering an array of lusciousness, that the ear is bemused into detecting scales and chords that never were on land or sea. What the exploratory eye subsequently discovers, perhaps, is no more than our stout and comfortable old friend, the highly well-born *hausfrau*, Mme. C Dur—with a vine leaf or two of C sharp minor or F major in her hair. The trick lies in the tone-color in the flabbergasting magic of the orchestration. There are moments in "Electra" when sounds come out of the orchestra that tug at the very roots of the hair, sounds so unearthly that they suggest a caroling of dragons or *bierfisch*—and yet they are made by the same old fiddles that play the Kaiser Quartet, and by the same old trombones that the Valkyrie ride like witches' broomsticks, and by the same old flutes that sob and snuffle in Tit'l's Serenade. And in parts of "Feuersnot"—but Roget must be rewritten by Strauss before "Feuersnot" is described. There is one place where the harps, taking a running start from the scrolls of the violins, leap slambang through (or is it into?) the firmament of heaven. Once, when I heard this passage played at a concert, a woman sitting beside me rolled over like a log, and had to be hauled out by the ushers.

Yes, Strauss is the boy to reorchestrate the symphonies of Schumann, particularly the B flat, the Rhenish and the fourth. I doubt that he could do much with Schubert, for

Schubert, though he is dead 88 years, yet remains curiously modern. The Unfinished symphony is full of exquisite color effects—consider, for example, the rustling figure for the strings in the first movement—and as for the C major, it is so stupendous a debauch of melodic and harmonic beauty that one scarcely notices the colors at all. In its slow movement mere loveliness in music probably says all that will ever be said . . . But what of old Ludwig? Har, har; here we begin pulling the whiskers of Baal Himself. Nevertheless, I am vandal enough to wonder, on sad Sunday mornings, what Strauss could do with the first movement of the C minor. More, if Strauss ever does it and lets me hear the result just once, I'll be glad to serve six months in jail with him . . . But in Munich, of course! And with a daily visitor's pass for Schwager Pschoor!

◇◇◇◇◇◇◇

Music After the War [2]

MUSICAL CRITICISM, in America confines itself chiefly to transient reviewing, and so the number of books by American critics is pitifully small. James Huneker has printed two or three good ones and W. J. Henderson and Henry Krehbiel have contributed a few punditic volumes, but after these the tale is soon told. Philip H. Goepp's three

---

[2] World War I.

volumes on the classical symphonies leave a great deal to be said. (Compare, for example, Sir George Grove's thick tome on Beethoven's nine.) Philip Hale's copious pedantries scarcely belong to criticism at all; besides, they are buried in the program books of the Boston Symphony Orchestra. As for Upton and other such fellows, they are mere agents of *Ladies' Home Journal* Kultur, and their tedious maunderings have little more value than the literary criticism of such empty sophomoralists as Hamilton Wright Mabie and Paul Elmer More. It is astonishing that Henderson has not been encouraged to reprint more of his New York *Sun* articles. They are not only full of novel ideas, but extremely well written—and good writing is quite as rare in musical criticism, both at home and abroad, as good writing in music. Henderson's books, however, have the air of being written down to a low level of stupidity. They are not aimed at musicians, but at singers, phonographists and the womens' clubs. Only Huneker has reached out for the sophisticated. He never explains the difference between a first violin and a second violin; he doesn't rehearse the plots of the Wagner music dramas; he always assumes that his readers, musically speaking, at least know their three R's.

In view of this paucity of music books by Americans, such a volume as "Music After the Great War", by Carl Van Vechten (*Schirmer*), takes on a considerable importance, despite its modest size and range. This Mr. Van Vechten, I believe, labors for New York *Times*, and is a prophet of the music of the future. Even Debussy begins to bore him; he has heard nothing interesting from that quarter for a long while. As for Germany, he finds it a desert, with Arnold Schoenberg behind the bar of its only inviting *gasthaus*. Richard Strauss? Pooh! Strauss is an exploded torpedo, a Zeppelin brought to earth; "he has nothing more to say." (Even the opening of the Alpine symphony, it would appear, is mere stick-candy.) England? Go to! Italy? Back to the barrel-organ! Where, then, is the *post-bellum* tone poetry to come from? According to Mr. Van Vechten, from Russia. It is the steppes that will produce it—or, more specifically, Prof. Igor Strawinsky, author of "The Nightingale" and of various revolutionary ballets. In the scores of Strawinsky, says Mr. Van Vechten, music takes a very large leap forward. Here, at last, we are definitely set free from melody and harmony; the thing becomes an ineffable complex of rhythms; "all rhythms are beaten into the ears."

New? Of the future? I have not heard these powerful shiverings and tremblings of M. Strawinsky, but I presume to doubt it none the less. "The ancient Greeks," says Mr. Van Vechten, "accorded rhythm a higher place than either melody or harmony." Well, what of it? So did the ancient Goths and Huns. So do the modern niggeroes and New Yorkers. The simple truth is that the accentuation of mere rhythm is a proof, not of progress in music, but of a reversion to barbarism. Rhythm is the earliest, the underlying element. The African savage beating his tom-tom, is content to go no further; the American composer of fox trots is with him. But music had scarcely any existence as an art-form until melody came to rhythm's aid, and its fruits were little save dullness until harmony began to support melody. To argue that mere rhythm, unsupported by anything save tone-color, may now take their place is to argue something so absurd that the mere statement is a sufficient answer to it.

The rise of harmony, true enough, laid open a dangerous field. Its exploration attracted meticulous minds; it was rigidly mapped in hard, geometrical forms; in the end it became almost unnavigable to the man of ideas. But no melodramatic rejection of all harmony is needed to work a reform. The business, indeed, is already gloriously under way. The dullest conservatory pupil has learned how to pull the noses of the old-time schoolmasters. No one cares a hoot any more about the ancient laws of preparation and resolution. (The rules grow so loose, indeed, that I may soon be tempted to write a tone-poem myself.) But out of this chaos new laws will inevitably arise, and though they will not be as rigid as the old ones, they will still be coherent and logical and intelligible. Already, in fact, gentlemen of professorial mind (to borrow from Dr. Sunday again) are doping them out; one needs but glance at such a book as René Lenormand's, to see that there is a certain order hidden in even the wildest vagaries of the moment. And when the boiling in the pot dies down, the truly great musicians will be found to be, not those who have been the most daring, but those who have been the most discreet and intelligent—those who have most skillfully engrafted what is good in the new upon what was sound in the old. Such a discreet fellow is Richard Strauss. His music is modern enough—but not too much. One is thrilled by its experiments and novelties, but at the same time one can enjoy it as music.

Haydn, Mozart, Beethoven and Wagner belonged to the same lodge. They were by no means the wildest revolutionaries of their days, but they were the best musicians. They didn't try to improve music by purging it of any of the elements that made it music; they tried, and with success, to give each element a new force and a new significance. Berlioz, I dare say, knew more about the orchestra than Wagner; he surely went further than Wagner in reaching out for new orchestral effects. But nothing he ever wrote has a fourth of the stability and value of "Tristan und Isolde." He was so intrigued by his tone-colors that he forgot his music. Wagner never got so befuddled.

MORE REVIEWS

꧁꧂

Ernest Newman and Others

Mencken's reviews of *A Musical Critic's Holiday*, by Ernest Newman
(New York: Alfred A. Knopf; 1925); *A Musical Motley*, by Ernest
Newman (New York: Alfred A. Knopf; 1925); *String Quartette Playing*,
by M. D. Herter Norton (New York: Carl Fischer); and *Music of the
Past*, by Wanda Landowska (New York: Alfred A. Knopf; 1924).
Appeared in *American Mercury*, December, 1925.

MR. NEWMAN calls his book a "holiday"; it really includes
the most valuable work that he, or any other critic writing
in English, has done in its field. For there are two things
in it that are rare and of great price, two qualities that are
as uncommon among music critics as they are among musicians: the first is sound, deep and well-ordered knowledge
of musical history, musical forms and idioms, musical anat-
omy and physiology, the second is simply common sense.
What a combination! How many music critics can show
even one of its two halves? What they deal with, ordinarily,
is merely the thing that is before them; what they have to
say of it is without background, without relevancy, without
roots. The conductor, it appears, took the first movement
of the Eroica too fast. The *Hexentanz* of the new genius,
Sascha Ganovski, is by Eric Satie out of "Roll, Jordan,

Roll." The new tenor sang flat, *i.e.* the Prohibition agent took a bribe, the movie wench said she loved her art, the dog had fleas. What is most music criticism? A banal and nonsensical discussion of performers, *i.e.*, of mountebanks, musical scullions, nonmusicians, enemies of music. The critic, exposed incessantly to their monkeyshines, takes on their character. He becomes a virtuoso. He gives his show— at the expense of music.

But not Newman. In "A Musical Critic's Holiday" he shows precisely everything that his average colleague lacks: an immense erudition, an astonishing skill at working his way through the tangled mazes of musical history—above all, the aforesaid sharp common sense. His business, in the book, is to examine scientifically the phenomena of musical development—to determine the qualities that make for genuine greatness in composers, and to find out what re-actions they arouse in contemporary taste—in brief, to dis-cover what hardships and impediments beset the first-rate man, and how he meets them. The result of that quest is a great slaughter of bombast and pretense. The neglected genius turns out to be an utter myth. He simply does not exist. There is no record in musical history of a man of the first talent who languished for recognition, or even lacked fame. "There has never yet been a composer so greatly in advance of his time that only an initiate here and there . . . could understand him." But what of the Schönbergs, the Stravinskys, the Ornsteins, the Saties? Such fowl have al-ways existed, world without end—and every generation has promptly forgotten those of the generation before.

Meanwhile, the Mozarts, the Beethovens, the Brahmses and the Wagners have gone marching on, honored while they lived, and remembered after they died. What have the tin-pot revolutionists left? Many a novelty, many an idea— and some of them good. But they survive today, woven into the fabric of music, not in the compositions of revolutionists, but in those of the men they stormed against— in brief, the genuinely first-rate composers of their time.

Mr. Newman's book is a work of great originality and high value. It sweeps away whole dumps of critical garbage. In "Musical Motley" he is less profound, but unfailingly amusing. "The Amateur Composer", "Bach in the Opera House", "Nonsense Music", "The Music of Death", "Brahms and the Waltz"—these are some of the things he discusses, always with something new to say, and always charmingly. There is charm, too, in Mme. Landowska's excellent volume upon eighteenth century music—charm and sound knowledge, for what she knows about the performance of it is deep and singular. More than charm is in Mrs. Norton's book on string quartette playing. The curious thing is that the volume was not written long ago. Are there any greater delights on this earth than those offered by chamber music? I don't mean merely listening to it; I mean playing it. Yet the literature for the guidance of performers is astonishingly meager, and the little that exists is of small value. Mrs. Norton indulges in no hollow rhapsodies. Instead she discusses the practical difficulties that quartette players confront, and shows how they are to be surmounted, with innumerable examples. Her experience has been wide, and she has got a great deal out of it beside mere virtuosity.

❖❖❖❖❖❖❖

The Poet and the Scientist

Mencken's reviews of *Music: A Science and an Art*, by John Redfield (New York: Alfred A. Knopf; 1928) and *Antheil and the Treatise on Harmony*, by Ezra Pound (Chicago: Pascal Covici; 1927). Appeared in *American Mercury*, August, 1928.

MR. POUND writes as a poet who is greatly interested in music, but has little technical knowledge of it; Mr. Redfield writes as a physicist who knows vastly more about it than most professional musicians. The difference in equipment shows itself in a difference of approach and method. Mr. Pound is somewhat rhetorical, and his discoveries are usually less astonishing than he plainly thinks they are; Mr. Redfield writes in an austerely scientific manner, but has more that is novel and apposite to say about the tone art than has been said by any other writer upon the subject for many years.

By this comparison, I hasten to add, I do not attempt to run down the effervescent Pound. He does his damndest, and it is surely not to be sniffed at. For a poet, and expecially an American poet, to have acquaintance with music at all is surely sufficiently unusual: perhaps it would not be going too far to put the prodigy beside Lindbergh's flight. Most of our native minnesingers, like most of our native artists in prose, seem to labor under the delusion that jazz is music, and some of them even appear to think that it is better than the music written by Beethoven. Pound nurses no such folly: he is well aware that jazz, with its relentless thumping in four-four time, is no more, at best, than an expanded drum part, with an accompaniment for wind-machines, most of them defective tonally. But though he thus rejects the brutal cacophony of Broadway, he embraces the almost equally brutal cacophony of George Antheil, and therein he proves, perhaps, that poets are at their best when they are writing poetry, and not when they are speculating about the other (and greater) fine arts.

Pound's chief discovery, in his "Treatise on Harmony", is that "any chord may be followed by any other, provided the right time interval be placed between them." This is the sort of dogma that seems revolutionary and portentous, but is in reality quite hollow. That the succession of chords is conditioned to some degree by the length of the har-monized notes has been known since the day of the first theorists. Every composer of any taste or skill takes the fact into consideration. Nor is it news that any chord may follow any other chord, given the proper dynamic and other conditions. Modulations more daring than any ever im-agined by Stravinsky have been made by boozy church organists for centuries, and without inflicting any appreci-able damage upon either pastor or congregation. The rules in the books were made to be broken, and perhaps the best way to estimate the true amperage of a composer—next, of course, to asking him what he thinks of Johann Strauss—is to observe the deftness and plausibility with which he

breaks them. Nor is there any visible sense in Pound's
notion that his hero, Antheil, has contributed something
to music by talking idiotically of "silences twenty minutes
long, *in the form*." This is pure bilge. A form with a hole
in it that large would simply be no form at all; as well talk
of a circle with a broken perimeter.

But though Pound thus fails as a musical revolutionist,
and Antheil with him, it must be said for both of them
that they are amusing fellows, and that what they have
to say on more conventional levels is frequently pungent
and judicious. Part of the book consists of a series of pro-
nunciamentos by Pound, with comments by Antheil.
Pound is usually more interesting than Antheil, for laymen
always write about music with more bounce and address
than musicians, but even Antheil sometimes verges upon
saying something. For example, when he allows that "one
must never be suddenly jarred in either a restaurant or a
concert hall," for "one eats food in the first and digests it
in the second." Thus, he concludes, "the average concert
and 'better' restaurant are identical." Again, there is his
dictum that "anyone with a capacity for grinning has a
'pleasing stage personality!'" Pound himself has some
incisive (if somewhat obvious) things to say about the
deficiencies of the piano, and the horrible effects that issue
out of playing it with the orchestra. On page 111 he writes
on form so sensibly that one suspects he must have forgotten, transiently, his nonsense about Antheil's "silences
twenty minutes long." And he has sound and penetrating
things to say about Mozart, Bach, Debussy, Chopin and

many another. His judgment upon Scriabin's grandiose "Poème d'Extase" deserves wide circulation. Scriabin, he says, would have been "kinder to his audience if he had labeled this poem 'Satire Upon an Old Gentleman', or possibly 'Confessions of an Old Gentleman in Trouble.' "

Mr. Redfield's book covers a wider range—in fact, almost the whole range of music. He was formerly a lecturer on the physics of music at Columbia, and has contributed a number of articles to The American Mercury. Here he discusses the nature of tone, the structure of the scale, the underlying laws of harmony, the aesthetic content of music, the methods of the piano-tuner, and the design of the various instruments of the orchestra. His pages are packed with novel ideas, and he maintains most of them with great plausibility. A great deal of the murkiness that one finds in the average *Harmonielehre*, he says, is due to the fact that C is wrongfully assumed to be the fundamental of the C major scale. The real fundamental, he believes, is F, and so on through the scales. In other words, we should abandon the Ionian mode and adopt the Lydian. Even so, he is not satisfied with our common scale, but proposes a new one of his own. His argument for this scale, is too technical to be summarized here, but it must be said for it that it is very impressive.

Mr. Redfield has much to say about the instruments of the orchestra, and proposes many changes in their design and combinations. He believes that the wood-wind has been unduly subordinated, and that there should be four or five times as many flutes as there are now. The theory that the violin, as it stands, is perfect does not convince him. Its physics deserves far more study than it has ever got; to this day no one seems to know the precise path of the vibrations of the bridge. He believes that the difference in quality and volume between the open and stopped tones could and should be remedied—"a problem for an engineer, not for a musician." He derides the common belief that the varnish of a violin has anything to do with determining its tone. If that were true, he says violin-makers would varnish the insides as well as the outsides of their instruments. Their hostility to change he ascribes to the fact that practically all of them are also dealers in old instruments, a very profitable business. If they produced better violins, it would destroy the high value of their present stocks.

The piano also comes in for an overhauling. Its chief defect today, aside from its bad tuning, which it shares with all other keyed instruments, lies in the fact that it cannot produce sustained tones. Its *staccato* is incomparable, but its *legato* is silly. Mr. Redfield sees no reason why this weakness should not be remedied. A simple enough electrical device might be used to sustain the tone, and even to increase or diminish it at will. As for the organ, it seems to be passing beyond the capacities of one performer. He now has two or three keyboards to manage, a row of pedals, and a huge battery of stops. It is no wonder that so many organists take to drink and die in the gutter. Mr. Redfield makes the plausible suggestion that it would be far better to have two performers to each organ, and suggests that they might be helped furthermore by various mechanical devices. As things stand, they frequently face such technical difficulties that their only recourse is to pull out all the stops and drown their blunders in a torrent of sound. If they had help it might be possible to increase the number of keys from twelve in an octave to thirty-five, and so get rid of the tempered scale. That would not only improve the organ itself, it would also improve choir singing, and so advance the Kingdom of God.

Mr. Redfield suggests many new instruments—a flute playing down to C in the bass clef, a couple of new fiddles between the violin and the 'cello, a contrabass clarinet in E flat, a new and lower trombone with a large helicon bell, a set of timpani capable of sounding the whole chromatic scale, and soprano and bass snare drums.[1] He believes that there are excellent possibilities in the xylophone, and the orchestral bells and marimba. All of them, he says, are much superior to "the dulcimer at the time Cristofori converted it into a piano by giving it a keyboard." The orchestral bells, in particular, attract him. He proposes that their solid bars be abandoned for pipes of the sort used in clocks and dinner-chimes, that resonator tubes and vibrator disks be provided, that piano hammers and dampers be added, and that a keyboard top the whole. "All the literature of the piano would be immediately available to be played upon it," and the result would be "the most ravishing sounds ever heard from a keyboard." Moreover, the new instrument

[1] High and low pitch snare drums, the contrabass clarinet and chromatic timpani, etc. are common today.

would probably cost a great deal less than a piano—and it would always be in tune.

I give a few samples from an extraordinarily thoughtful and interesting book. Mr. Redfield has more to say than any of the usual musical theorists. His ideas are supported by a great body of exact knowledge, and he writes with great clarity and charm.

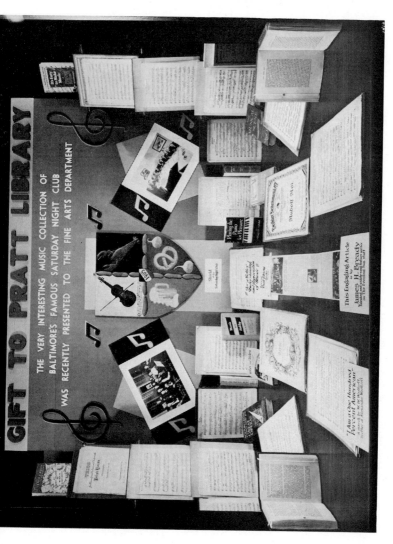

PLATE X · *Enoch Pratt Free Library's window display of some of the music from the Saturday Night Club's library. The club shield is in the center*

OCCUPATIONAL
HAZARD

❦

Music as a Trade

From the *Smart Set*, June, 1922, p. 46. Included in A MENCKEN CHRESTOMATHY, 1949, pp. 547–8.

MUSIC IS enormously handicapped as an art by the fact that its technique is so frightfully difficult. I do not refer, of course, to the technique of the musical executant, but to that of the composer. Any literate man can master the technique of poetry or the novel in ten days, and that of the drama—despite all the solemn hocus-pocus of the professors who presume to teach it—in three weeks, but not even the greatest genius could do a sound fugue without long and painful preparation. To write even a string quartet is not merely an act of creation, like writing a sonnet; it is also an act of applied science, like cutting out a set of tonsils. I know of no other art that demands so elaborate a professional training. The technique of painting has its difficulties, particularly in the direction of drawing, but a hundred men master them for one who masters counterpoint.

So with sculpture. Perhaps the art which comes nearest to music in technical difficulties is architecture—that is, modern architecture. As the Greeks practiced it, it was relatively simple, for they used simple materials and avoided all delicate problems of stress and strain; and they were thus able to keep their whole attention upon pure design. But the modern architect, with his complex mathematical and mechanical problems, must be an engineer before he is an artist, and the sort of engineering that he must master bristles with technical snares and conundrums. The serious musician is an even worse case. Before he may write at all he must take in and coordinate a body of technical knowledge that is about as great as the outfit of an astronomer.

I say that all this constitutes a handicap on the art of music. What I mean is that it snares off many men who have charming musical ideas and would make good composers, but who have no natural talent or taste for the technical groundwork. For one Schubert who overcomes the handicap by sheer genius there must be dozens who are repelled and discouraged. There is another, and perhaps even worse disadvantage. The potential Schuberts flee in alarm, but the Professor Jadassohns march in bravely. That is to say, music is hard for musicians, but easy for pedants and quacks. Its constant invasion by tinpot revolutionists is the result. It offers an inviting playground to the jackass whose delight it is to astonish the bourgeoisie with insane feats of virtuosity.

◇◇◇◇◇◇◇

The Reward of the Artist

From Damn! a book of calumny (P. Goodman; 1918).

A MAN LABORS and fumes for a whole year to write a symphony in G minor. He puts enormous diligence into it, and much talent, and maybe no little downright genius. It draws his blood and wrings his soul. He dies in it that he may live again. Nevertheless, its final value, in the open market of the world, is a great deal less than that of a fur overcoat, or a handful of authentic hair from the whiskers of Henry Wadsworth Longfellow.

LITTLE
CONCERT-HALLS

ᙏᙏ

From the *American Mercury*, March 28, 1930; under pseudonym of
Atwood C. Bellamy.

WHAT THE Little Theaters have done for the drama in
America is known to everyone. If there is any hospitality
to intelligence on Broadway today it is mainly due to them.
Without them the commercial managers would still be in
the Erlanger-Frohman-Belasco stage of evolution, and the
best plays of the day would be such things as "Zaza" and
"The Lion and the Mouse." These Little Theaters, at the
start, had hard sledding, both in New York and in the
provinces. All the head men of the theater were against
them, and so were nearly all the dramatic critics. They
found it difficult to obtain suitable plays; [1] they found it
even more difficult to discover competent performers; they
were made fun of on every hand. But now all that is
changed. They have an enormous repertory of plays to

---

[1] In 1909 Mencken wrote a one-act satire on a musical subject,
"The Artist," which was performed in Little Theaters in several
cities. It was subsequently translated into French, Danish and
German.

choose from, and they have trained their own actors. And everyone speaks well of them, including even the more enlightened of the commercial managers.

I rise to suggest that what has thus worked so well with the drama might work just as well with music. That is to say, I propose that Little Concert-Halls be set up everywhere—not only in New York, but in all the cities and towns of the land. And I propose that, like the Little Theaters, they be devoted to putting on what is not now done commercially, and that they be directed and operated, not by the professionals who now burden American music, but by amateurs. I propose that these amateurs not only run them, but also play in them, just as the amateurs of two decades ago played in the Little Theaters. And I propose, finally, that they be run, not for profit, but for the simple love of music.

I can see no reason why the scheme should not be workable. To put on opera takes millions and to put on symphony concerts takes almost as much, but to put on a string quartette takes next to nothing. Specifically, it takes a platform about as big as an ordinary dining-room, and space for fifty or sixty spectators—that is all. Throw two parlors into one, and you have it. Clean out the loft above what was once a horse-stable, and you have it again. Rent an old store in a side street, and you have it once more.

The chamber music that is now heard in the United States is usually heard under the worst possible conditions. There are very few public halls suitable for it, and so it is forced into halls that are not suitable for it. I myself

have heard the Flonzaley Quartette try to play Haydn's
E flat, opus 20, in a hall in which Sousa's band had played
the week before. And another time I heard Ysaÿe and two
others tackle the first Brahms trio in a hall so wide and long
and high that, sitting in the middle of it, I felt like an
electron lost in a molecule. It goes without saying that the
acoustics of such barns are not adapted to quartette playing.
Yet most of the quartette playing that goes on in America
goes on in them.

Chamber music is precisely what its name implies: it
is music intended to be played in ordinary rooms—not
small ones, perhaps, but still ordinary rooms. It never
sounds so well as when one is close to it. Probably the ideal
place, when the composition is a quartette, is directly in
the middle of the four players. Retreat forty feet, and at
once the thing begins to be thin and wheezy. Go back sixty
feet, and one may well leave the place altogether. The
chamber music classics were all written for small halls and
small audiences. When Beethoven or Mozart or Schubert
wanted to make a lot of noise and fill a big hall, he turned
to the full orchestra.

My first point is that a hall exactly suitable for chamber
music—up to and including such things as Schubert's and
Mendelssohn's octettes—may be obtained in any American
town for no more rent a month than it takes to keep a car,
and that furnishing it would cost scarcely more than a good
suit of clothes. My second point is that, if amateurs be
counted in, there are players enough to man it almost everywhere—and audiences ready to listen to them. That so

little chamber music is heard in America today is not the fault of the audiences. It is the fault of the system that converts a string quartette into a sort of travelling circus, and puts it to playing in halls big enough for horse-shows, that the rapacity of whole packs of managers, booking agents, local managers, house managers, press-agents and other such hangers-on may be satisfied.

The Little Concert-Halls that I have in mind would bear no such burden. It would not be open every night, and it would not be dependent on the box-office. Its heart and soul would be the performers. They would use it for rehearsals, and, when they got good enough, they would ask the public in to listen. There would be seats for fifty, a hundred, maybe two hundred—no more. And the next night some other group would play, maybe with some of the same performers appearing again, and maybe with a whole new outfit. One night—string quartettes. The next night—trios or a sonata evening. The next week—quintettes (say Brahms' or Mozart's for clarinet and strings, and Schubert's "Forellen"), or maybe a pair of sextettes (say Dvořák's and Raff's!), or a mixture of big things and little. Once or twice a year—a whole evening for the Schubert octette, or a programme of pieces for salon orchestra.

I see no reason why it should be difficult, in any sizeable American town, to raise the money for such an enterprise. There is no need to have a hall on main street, with electric lights outside and a doorman dressed like a field marshal. There is no need to have a paid manager or to do any advertising. There is even no need to pay the performers, save maybe now and then, when a bassoon or a clarinet is called for, and no amateur who can play it is to be found. The Little Theaters all started on shoe-strings. They went up alleys and kept to themselves. The fun was for the performers and their friends, not for people wandering around idly, vacillating between this and that movie show. But a public soon found them out, and presently many of them were making their expenses, and not a few were even accumulating capital. Such a hall as I have in mind may be rented, even in the big cities, for no more than $1,000 a year. Add $500 for light, heat, programmes, music, and other current expenses, and $500 for the unforeseen, and the total is still within the means of any average group of twenty or thirty music-lovers. Say that twenty performances are given during the season, and that an average of a hundred tickets is sold for each, at $1 a piece; the cost is now precisely nothing. But even if there is a deficit, what true amateur, considering all the fun he has had, will object to paying his share of it?

In this department of finance, the experience of the Little Theaters ought to be useful. I don't know how they managed it, but manage it they did. The death-rate, of course, was very high among them, but some of them always survived, and whenever one of them fell out another was ready to take its place. Their work completely changed the attitude of the American public toward the drama. Today it would roar with laughter over things that it gaped at in all solemnity twenty years ago. And today it is paying to see plays that it once ignorantly snickered at.

The same might be done for music, and especially for chamber music, which is the loveliest kind there is. No great capital is needed, and no tedious propaganda. The materials are everywhere, and also, I believe, the interest. All that is necessary is to give it a chance to show itself. I'd like to see a Little Concert-Hall in every town in the United States, and in the big cities scores of them. And some day, I believe I'll see them.

"LIGHT" MOTIFS

⊰◈⊱

On Tenors

From the Baltimore *Sun*, November 10, 1907.

LIKE THE red-haired girl and the mother-in-law, the church choir tenor is a butt for every cretinous punster and village humorist. His low notes are declared to be off the key; his skyscrapers are compared to the unearthly shrieks of a dissipated oboe. He is held up to the public scorn and odium. And now, to add to his woes, one of these silly Western college professors springs into the limelight with the "discovery" that the tenor voice is not a voice at all, but a disease. When the healthy male throat makes noises, says the professor, those noises are of baritone or bass variety. The man who sings tenor needs medicine. His vocal chords are loose.

We have no faith whatever in this alleged "discovery." It has an air of improbability and absurdity. It stands opposed to known and admitted facts. That the act of singing tenor is a tort, or outrage, we do not presume to deny, but moral turpitude, as everyone knows, differs vastly from psychological abnormality. A tort differs from a lesion.

A crime is no brother to a broken leg. And so we hold that the average tenor needs, not medicine, but religion—not a trained nurse, but a turnkey.

The tenor voice differs as much from all other human voices as the French horn differs from a piccolo. It has more wolf tones, and it is, in the true sense, a transposing instrument. The ordinary scale handicaps and embarrasses it. A scale made up entirely of diminished sevenths, if such a thing were possible, would fit it better. It is a voice ineffable and unearthly. In its upper register (particularly when it appears with other voices, in an *a capella* chorus) it grabs the heart strings and tears them out by the roots.

We admit, of course, that there are many robust tenors whose singing is very pleasant and frequently musical. One such is M. Enrico Caruso. And there are others too. But the average amateur tenor can urge no such excuse for himself. His singing is entirely and utterly indefensible. His high B flat is wedged somewhere between A natural and G sharp. His grimaces are horrific. His breathing is as vociferously obvious as the cough of a gas engine.

Let him be anathema!

Mysteries of the Tone-Art

From the Baltimore *Evening Sun*, July 1, 1910.

. . . To PLAY THE 'CELLO one must be sound in wind and limb, and the 'cello, on its part, pays back, with interest, the muscular energy expended in performing upon it. Remove the vestments of a veteran 'cello player and you will find muscles as round and as hard as mock oranges. The *extensor carpi radialis longior,* in the upper right arm, stands out like an Ionic pillar in front of a colonial home. And in the lower arm the *flexor sublimis digitorum* has the thickness of a piano leg and the unyielding texture of a clarinetist's intellect.

Some psychophysiologist should give earnest study to the effects of the various orchestral instruments upon the persons affecting them. Why is it, for example, that most oboe players are men of violent temper? It has been found in Germany that 8 per cent of all crimes of violence committed by musicians are to be laid to oboe players, though they constitute less than one per cent of the whole body of performers. A recent census of Bavaria showed that of the 359 oboe players in that Kingdom, 43 were anarchists and 161 were militant socialists. It is generally believed by other musicians that the plaintive, unearthly note of the oboe is to blame for the eccentricities of its performers. The other men of the orchestra commonly object to sitting next to the oboes. They say that the noise disturbs them and makes them play out of tune.

It would also be interesting to find out why all performers upon the viola are pessimists and all double bass players such heavy drinkers. Alcohol seems to have no effect whatever upon an experienced double bass player. There is one man in the Gewandhaus orchestra at Leipzig whose daily potation consists of 18 liters of Munich *dunkle,* almost enough to paralyze a whole lodge of Elks. And yet he is always sober, alert and accurate in his playing. He is, indeed, the only double bass player in all Germany who can get through the scherzo of Beethoven's Fifth Symphony without once stopping to remove the rosin dust from his eyes.

❖❖❖❖❖❖❖

Masters of Tone

From the *Smart Set*, May, 1912, p. 158; in A MENCKEN CHRESTOMATHY, 1949, p. 550.

WAGNER—The rape of the Sabines . . . a *kommers* in Olympus.

Beethoven—The glory that was Greece . . . the grandeur that was Rome . . . a laugh.

Haydn—A seidel on the table . . . a girl on your knee . . . another and different girl in your heart.

Chopin—Two embalmers at work upon a minor poet . . . the scent of tuberoses . . . Autumn rain.

Richard Strauss—Old Home Week in Gomorrah.

Johann Strauss—Forty couples dancing . . . one by one they slip from the hall . . . sounds of kisses . . . the lights go out.

Puccini—Silver macaroni, exquisitely tangled.

Debussy—A pretty girl with one blue eye and one brown one.

Bach—Genesis I, I.

MORALS
AND MUSIC

❧❦❧

Music and Sin

From Prejudices, fifth series, 1926, pp. 293–6.

. . . The delusion seems to persist that jazz is highly aphrodisiacal. I never encounter a sermon on the subject without finding it full of dark warnings to parents, urging them to keep their nubile daughters out of the jazz palaces on the ground that the voluptuous music will inflame their passions and so make them easy prey to bond salesmen, musicians and other such carnal fellows. All this seems to me to be nonsense. Jazz, in point of fact, is not voluptuous at all. Its monotonous rhythms and puerile tunes make it a sedative rather than a stimulant. If it is an aphrodisiac, then the sound of riveting is also aphrodisiac. What fetches the flappers who come to grief in the jazz parlors is not the music at all, but the alcohol. Drinking it out of flasks in the washrooms, they fail to keep the dose in harmony with their natural resistance, and so they lose control of their faculties, and what follows is lamentable. Jazz, which came

in with Prohibition, gets the blame that belongs to its partner. In the old days, when it was uncommon for refined
women to get drunk at dances, it would have been quite
harmless. To-day even Chopin's funeral march would be
dangerous.

The truth is that jazz is probably the least voluptuous
variety of music commonly heard in Christendom. There
are plenty of Methodist hymns that are ten times as aphrodisiacal, and the fact is proved by the scandals that follow
every camp-meeting. In most parts of the United States,
indeed, the Methodists have begun to abandon camp-
meetings as subversive of morality. Where they still flourish
it is not unusual for even the rev. clergy to be taken in
Byzantine practices. But so-called good music is yet worse
than the Methodist hymns. Has the world so soon forgotten James Huneker's story of the prudent opera mamma
who refused to let her daughter sing Isolde, on the ground
that no woman could ever get through the second act without forgetting God? That second act, even so, is much overestimated. There are piano pieces of Chopin that are a
hundred times worse; if the Comstocks really had any sense,
they would forbid their performance. And what of the late
Puccini? If "La Bohème" is not an aphrodisiac, then what
is? Yet it is sung publicly all over the world. Only in
Atlanta, Ga., is there a law against it, and even that law was
probably inspired by the fact that it was written by a Catholic and not by the fact that it has brought hundreds of
thousands of Christian women to the abyss.

Old Ludwig himself was not without guilt. His "Egmont"

overture is a gross and undisguised appeal to the *medulla oblongata*. And what of his symphonies and quartettes? The last movement of his Eroica is not only voluptuous to the last degree; it is also Bolshevistic. Try to play it with your eyes on a portrait of Dr. Calvin Coolidge. You will find the thing as impossible as eating ice cream on roast beef. At the time of its first performance in Vienna the moral sense of the community was so greatly outraged that Beethoven had to get out of town for a while. I pass over Wagner, whose "Tristan und Isolde" was probably his most decorous work, despite Huneker—think of "Parsifal"! —and come to Richard Strauss! Here I need offer no argument: his "Salome" and "Elektra" have been prohibited by the police, at one time or another, in nearly every country in the world. I believe "Der Rosenkavalier" is still worse, though the police leave it unmolested. Compare its first act to the most libidinous jazz ever heard of on Broadway. It is like comparing vodka to ginger-pop. No woman who hears it is ever the same again. She may remain within the law, but her thoughts are wayward henceforth. Into her ear the sirens have poured their abominable song. She has been beset by witches. There is a sinister glitter in her eye.

◇◇◇◇◇◇◇◇

The Music-Lover

From *The Allied Arts*, PREJUDICES: SECOND SERIES, 1920, pp. 194–6.
First printed in the *Smart Set*, December, 1919, pp. 70–1.

OF ALL FORMS of the uplift, perhaps the most futile is that which addresses itself to educating the proletariat in music. The theory behind it is that a taste for music is an elevating passion, and that if the great masses of the plain people could only be inoculated with it they would cease to herd into the moving-picture parlors, or to listen to demagogues, or to beat their wives and children. The defect in this theory lies in the fact that such a taste, granting it to be elevating—which, pointing to professional musicians, I certainly deny—simply cannot be implanted. Either it is born in a man or it is not born in him. If it is, then he will get gratification from it at whatever cost—he will hear music if Hell freezes over. But if it isn't, then no amount of education will ever change him—he will remain indifferent until the last sad scene on the gallows.

No child who has this congenital taste ever has to be urged or tempted or taught to love music. It takes to tone inevitably and irresistibly; nothing can restrain it. What is more, it always tries to make music, for the delight in sounds is invariably accompanied by a great desire to produce them. All genuine music-lovers try to make music. They may do it badly, and even absurdly, but nevertheless they do it. Any man who pretends to cherish the tone-art and yet has never learned the scale of C major—any and every such man is a fraud. The opera-houses of the world are crowded with such liars. You will even find hundreds of them in the concert-halls, though here the suffering they have to undergo to keep up their pretense is almost too much for them to bear. Many of them, true enough, deceive themselves. They are honest in the sense that they credit their own buncombe. But it is buncombe none the less.

In the United States the number of genuine music-lovers is probably very low. There are whole States, e.g., Alabama, Arkansas and Idaho, in which it would be difficult to muster a hundred. In New York, I venture, not more than one person in every thousand of the population deserves to be counted. The rest are, to all intents and purposes, tone deaf. They cannot only sit through the infernal din made by the current jazz-bands; they actually like it. This is precisely as if they preferred the works of the Duchess to those of Thomas Hardy, or the paintings of the men who make covers for the magazines to those of El Greco. Such persons inhabit the sewers of the bozart. No conceivable education could rid them of their native infirmity. They are born incurable.

POTPOURRI

THE HAPSBURGS seem to be quite down and out. The arch-dukes of the house, once so steadily in the newspapers, are now heard of no longer, and the Emperor Karl appears to be a jackass almost comparable to an American Congressman. But what a family in the past! To one member Haydn dedicated the Kaiser quartette, to another Beethoven dedicated the Erzherzog trio, and to a third old Johann Strauss dedicated the Kaiser waltz. Match that record in all human history. (*Smart Set*, November, 1921, p. 36; A *Mencken Chrestomathy*, p. 219: Undying Glories)

. . . If it were possible to produce a Chopin with a few doses of *tubercle bacilli*, even at the cost of killing him at thirty-nine, it would surely be worth while. And if a technique is ever worked out for producing a Beethoven, or even making measurably more likely the production of a Beethoven, with any other pathogenic organisms, then certainly only idiots will complain if they kill him at fifty-seven. (*Smart Set*, December, 1919, pp. 66–7; A *Mencken Chrestomathy*, p. 369: Pathological Note)

A man who has taken aboard two or three cocktails is less competent than he was before to steer a battleship down Ambrose Channel, or to cut off a leg, or to draw up a deed of trust, or to conduct Bach's B minor Mass, but he is immensely more competent to entertain a dinner party, or to admire a pretty girl, or to *hear* Bach's B minor Mass. (*American Mercury*, February, 1924, pp. 201–3; *Prejudices, Fourth Series*, 1924, pp. 173–9; *A Mencken Chrestomathy*, pp. 388–9: Portrait of an Ideal World)

Beethoven suffered more during the composition of the Fifth symphony than all the judges on the benches of the world have suffered jointly since the time of Pontius Pilate. (New York *Evening Mail*, November 16, 1917, *Prejudices, Second Series*, 1920, pp. 155–71; *A Mencken Chrestomathy*, p. 446: The Divine Afflatus)

There is no more confining work known to man than instrumentation. The composer who has spent a day at it is invariably nervous and ill. For hours his body is bent over his music-paper, the while his pen engrosses little dots upon thin lines. I have known composers, after a week or so of such labor, to come down with auto-intoxication in its most virulent forms. Perhaps the notorious ill health of Beethoven, and the mental breakdowns of Schumann, Tschaikowsky and Hugo Wolf had their origin in this direction. (New York *Evening Mail*, November 16, 1917; *Prejudices, Second Series*, 1920, pp. 155–71; *A Mencken Chrestomathy*, p. 447: The Divine Afflatus)

. . . Poetry is a comforting piece of fiction set to more or less lascivious music—a slap on the back in waltz time—a grand release of longings and repressions to the tune of flutes, harps, sackbuts, psalteries and the usual strings. (*Smart Set*, June, 1920, pp. 138–43; *Prejudices, Third Se-*

ries, 1922, pp. 150–70; *A Mencken Chrestomathy*, p. 449:
The Poet and His Art)

Poetry that is all music is obviously relatively rare, for
only a poet who is also a natural musician can write it, and
natural musicians are much rarer in the world than poets.
(*Smart Set*, June, 1920, pp. 138–43; *Prejudices*, *Third
Series*, 1922, pp. 150–70; *A Mencken Chrestomathy*, p. 451:
The Poet and His Art)

I have heard each of the first eight symphonies of Beethoven more than fifty times, and most of Mozart's, Haydn's,
Schubert's and Schumann's quite as often. Yet if Beethoven's C minor were announced for performance tonight, I'd
surely go to hear it. More, I'd enjoy every instant of it. Even
second-rate music has this lasting quality. Some time ago
I heard Johann Strauss' waltz, "Geschichten aus dem
Wiener Wald," for the first time in a long while. I knew it
very well in my goatish days, every note of it was familiar.
Nevertheless, it gave me immense delight. Imagine a man
getting delight out of a painting of corresponding caliber—
a painting already so familiar to him that he could repro-
duce it from memory. (*Smart Set*, January, 1921, pp. 39–40;
Prejudices, *Fourth Series*, 1924, pp. 240–8; *A Mencken
Chrestomathy*, p. 552: Hand-Painted Oil Paintings)

As for a human being incapable of writing passable verse,
he simply does not exist. It is done, as everyone knows, by
children—and sometimes so well that their poems are
printed in books and quite solemnly reviewed. But good
music is never written by children—and I am not forgetting
Mozart, Schubert and Mendelssohn. Music belongs to the

very latest stage of culture; to compose it in the grand manner requires painful training, and the highest sort of natural skill. It is complex, delicate, difficult. A miraculous youth may show talent for it, but he never reaches anything properly describable as mastery of it until he is mature. The music that all of us think of when we think of the best was written by men a bit bent by experience. And so with prose. Prose has no stage scenery to hide behind. It is spontaneous, but must be fabricated by thought and painstaking. Prose is the ultimate flower of the art of words. Next to music, it is the finest of all the fine arts. (*Smart Set*, January, 1921, pp. 39–40; *Prejudices, Fourth Series*, 1924, pp. 240–8; A *Mencken Chrestomathy*, pp. 553–4: Hand-Painted Oil Paintings)

MUSICAL
ALLUSIONS TO
AUTHORS

⚜

Is DREISER actually deaf to their dreadful cacophony?
(*American Mercury*, March, 1926, pp. 379–81—review of
An American Tragedy, by Theodore Dreiser; *A Mencken
Chrestomathy*, p. 504)

I try to give you, ineptly and grotesquely, some notion of
the talk of the man, but I must fail inevitably. It was, in
brief, chaos, and chaos cannot be described, but it was chaos
drenched in all the colors imaginable, chaos scored for an
orchestra which made the great band of Berlioz seem like a
fife and drum corps. (*Century*, June, 1921, pp. 191–7;
Prejudices, Third Series, 1922, pp. 65–83; *A Mencken
Chrestomathy*, p. 512: Huneker: A Memory)

There is in "Heart of Darkness" a perfection of design
which one encounters only rarely and miraculously in prose
fiction: it belongs rather to music. I can't imagine taking

a single sentence out of that stupendous tale without leaving a visible gap; it is as thoroughly *durch componiert* as a fugue. And I can't imagine adding anything to it, even so little as a word, without doing it damage. As it stands it is austerely and beautifully perfect, just as the slow movement of the Unfinished Symphony is perfect. (*Smart Set*, December, 1922, pp. 141–4; *Prejudices, Fifth Series*, 1926, pp. 34–41; *A Mencken Chrestomathy*, p. 520: Joseph Conrad)

What the enigmatical Pole has to offer is something quite different. If its parallel is to be found in music, it is not in Schubert, but in Beethoven—perhaps even more accurately in Johann Sebastian Bach. (*Smart Set*, December, 1922, pp. 141–4; *Prejudices, Fifth Series*, 1926, pp. 34–41; *A Mencken Chrestomathy*, p. 518: Joseph Conrad)

FROM A LETTER
TO ISAAC GOLDBERG

❦

(May 6, 1925)

OF MY TASTES in music: in the main they are very orthodox.
I put Beethoven first, even ahead of Bach—mainly, I suppose, because I have heard more of him than Bach. It
seems to me that the first movement of the Eroica, Beethoven's first formal defiance of the old symphonic music, remains unparalleled today. Even Beethoven never wrote
anything more colossal. The funeral march following seems
to me to be, by contrast, almost banal. But of all the Beethoven symphonies I like No. 8 best. It is light but anyone who
regards it as trivial is simply a damned fool. Two things
attract me to Beethoven: first, his immense dignity; second,
his superb workmanship. He is never hollow and sentimental—and he makes more of a few bald notes than most
composers make of first-rate melodic ideas. Consider the
first movement of the Fifth and the slow movement of the
Seventh. He is the musical scientist par excellence. He never
trusts to mere inspiration. All his effects are achieved by
sheer brain power.

Next to Beethoven, as a master of the larger forms, I put Brahms. His first symphony is almost incomparable. Incomparable? Then what of his second and fourth? Two masterpieces! I like his third rather less. His "Deutches Requiem" belongs in the front rank of choral works. I put it beside Bach's B minor Mass. Compared to it, all the familiar oratorios are shabby stuff, fit only for Methodists. Early in life Brahms wrote a trio, opus 8. I believe that its first subject is one of the most beautiful melodies ever written. Only Schubert ever went beyond it.

Of Schubert I hesitate to speak. The fellow was scarcely human. His merest belch was as lovely as the song of the sirens. He sweated beauty as naturally as a Christian sweats hate. What I marvel at is the neglect of some of his best music, for example, the Tragische Symphonie. Its slow movement is certainly almost as good as the slow movement of the Unfinished. Yet it is seldom played. So with his trios and his other piano music. I once traveled 80 miles to hear his octette. The horn player failed to show up, and I had to play his part on a piano. His quintette, opus 163, is another masterpiece. His two piano trios, op. 99 and 100, are both too long—but what fine stuff is in them! Take a look at their slow movements. Schubert's songs I have heard, of course, but I greatly dislike singing, and so I enjoy them less than I ought to. There is more music in his "Deutsche Tänze" than in the whole of Debussy. The fact that these little waltzes and Ländler are very simple deceives many. But so is the Parthenon simple.

Of Mozart I say little. Like Schubert, he is beyond critical analysis: he simply happened. Why are his smaller symphonies so little played? At least six of them are perfect. The big orchestras apparently play only the Jupiter and the G minor. In the same way most of the Haydn symphonies are forgotten. Everything that Haydn wrote, including especially his string quartettes, should be played publicly at least once a year in every civilized city of the world. It would make people ashamed of listening to the maudlin obscenities of Stravinsky and company.

Of Schumann I like best his first and fourth symphonies. The second seems dull to me. The third lacks coherence, though it is very lovely in spots. Mendelssohn I like in spots,—for example, the scherzo of the Scotch symphony. I greatly admire a number of second-raters: among them Goldmark and Dvořák. Goldmark knew how to be sentimental without shedding crocodile tears. Dvořák wrote a great deal of fine stuff in the smaller forms—for example, his Slavonic Dances. I think they are much better than the Hungarian Dances of Brahms—more ingenious and far more beautiful.

Of the men still alive, I believe that Richard Strauss is easily the first. He is the only man who has offered a serious challenge to Wagner as a dramatic composer—I don't mean a theater composer. He builds up a climax with intense skill, and handles the orchestra better even than Wagner. His music is not often lovely, but it is always moving. But he knows how to write a tune—when he wants to. The first act of "Der Rosenkavalier" is worth all the Italian operas ever written. Of all his work, I prefer "Electra" and "Tod und Verklärung." I also like such parts of "Feuersnot" as I have heard; unfortunately, I don't know the whole opera.

Wagner was probably the best musician who ever lived, as Schubert was the greatest genius who ever wrote music. His command of his materials was unmatched in his time, and has never been surpassed, save by Richard Strauss. His ideas, of course, were infinitely better than Strauss'. In "Tristan und Isolde," for example, he displays so many, and they are so good, that the effect is almost stupefying. I believe that "Die Meistersinger" is the greatest single work of art ever produced by man. It took more skill to plan and write it than it took to plan and write the whole canon of Shakespeare. Wagner's defect is that he is often theatrical, and hence a mountebank. Think of the Char-Feitag music in "Parsifal." It actually describes a romantic but plainly illegal act of love.

Puccini, I believe, has been underestimated. He was the best of the wops. His aim was to entertain well-fed folk after dinner—and he did it very competently. "La Bohème" is surely not a great work, but anyone who fails to get pleasure out of it must be tone-deaf. Verdi, I believe, is not to be heard sober, but with a few whiskies under my belt I enjoy the last act of "Il Trovatore." Chopin is another composer who is best heard after seeing a bootlegger. His music is excellent on rainy afternoons in Winter, with the fire burning, the shaker full, and the girl somewhat silly.

The so-called moderns interest me very much, for I am fond of experiments in the arts. But I'd rather read their music than hear it. It always fails to come off: it is *Augenmusik.*[1]

So far as I can make out, Stravinsky never had a musical idea in his life—that is, in the sense that Schubert and Mozart had them. He makes up for his lack of them by tuning his fiddle strings to G flat, D sharp, B and B sharp, and playing above the bridge. That such preposterous rubbish is solemnly heard and applauded is sufficient proof that a sucker is born every minute. I believe that not more than 10% of the people who go to concerts are actually interested in music, or get any genuine pleasure out of it. They are simply interested in mountebanks, i.e., fiddlers, caterwaulers, conductors, etc. When the composer happens to be a mountebank also they are doubly pleased.

I never go to hear virtuosi if I can help it. Even Kreisler tires me after an hour. It offends me greatly to see a performer getting applause that belongs to the composer. I take little interest in conductors, though I know a number of them and like them as men. Their importance is immensely overestimated. A flute player with a severe Katzenjammer can do more to spoil a concert than even a Damrosch. Of all the conductors I am familiar with I like Muck the best. He is a good musician and respects composers. His conducting is intelligent, painstaking and in good taste. He

[1] One wonders what he would say today of the current trend to "dehumanize" music: of Anton von Webern's scientific and super-contrived compositions, Stockhausen's music of chance and Davidovsky's electronic etudes.

does not give a show; he plays the music. His competence naturally made him unpopular with frauds who constitute a majority of Boston Orchestra audiences, and at the first chance, during the late war, they fell on him. Some time ago I heard the Boston Orchestra in New York, under Koussevitsky. It was like meeting a beautiful woman of the year 1900—now middle-aged, simpering, and hideously frescoed.

I seldom go to the opera; it is to music what a bawdy house is to a cathedral. The spectacle of fat women sweating, with their mouths wide open, is very offensive. I believe that most of the best music written is in the form of symphonies for grand orchestra; I'd rather hear it than any other kind. I greatly enjoy chamber music, especially when I am helping to play it. I believe, with Franz Kneisel, that most string quartettes would be improved if they had parts for bull fiddles, and were quintettes. Some of the loveliest music in the world is written for string quartettes—but it inevitably begins to sound thin after half an hour or so. Too much of the music is above middle C.

I know very little about piano music, and seldom play the piano alone. Piano music, in the main, seems to me to lack dignity. Even the Beethoven Sonatas fall below old Ludwig's usual level. But maybe I underestimate them because most of them are beyond my technique. That may also explain my feeling that Chopin is a sugar-teat. As a boy I used to like Moskowski. I got over it when I began to smoke.

French music, in the main, does not stir me; it is pretty, but trashy. I believe that Vincent D'Indy is one of the worst composers ever heard of, with Massenet close upon his heels. Bizet I like very much better; he at least did not simper. I like some of the New Russian music—I mean, of course, the pre-Stravinskian music. Tschaikovsky, when he tried to be solemn, became merely bombastic, but he could write lovely tunes, and he put many of them into his smaller stuff, for example, the Casse-Noisette suite. He should have written fewer symphonies [2] and more waltzes. Which brings me to Johann Strauss. I believe that he was a musician of the first caliber—a man vastly more talented than, say Mendelssohn. "Geschichten aus dem Wiener Wald" is not merely good; it is a masterpiece. Beethoven would have admired it, as Wagner, Schumann and Brahms admired it.

Why German music should be so much better than any other kind I don't know. I have often wondered. The English, theoretically, should be good musicians. They have good ears, as their poetry shows, and they excel at teamwork. But most of their music, at least in our time, is palpably fourth-rate. They never get beyond a pretty amateurishness. All their genuinely good composers are non-English—for example, Sullivan (a man of very great talent) and Delius. There are, indeed, only two kinds of music: German music and bad music.

I have spoken evilly of French music. I except, of course,

---

[2] H. L. Mencken has flatly called The Sixth Symphony (Tschaikovsky's) the "Homosexual Tragedy." (See *Men of Music* by Brockway and Weinstock. New York: Simon and Schuster; 1939, p. 491.)

that of Cesar Frank. He was a man of immense talent. But I deny that he was a Frenchman, or that he wrote anything properly describable as French music. He was, in fact, scarcely more a Frenchman than Händel was an Englishman. But Berlioz? Well, I'll give you Berlioz. But did he write any music?

Jazz? It may be defined briefly as the sort of music that the persons who go to the opera really like. A few amusing ingenuities are in it; it is clever in the same sense that a caricature may be clever. Some day a composer of genuine talent will put a jazz scherzo into a symphony. A hundred years hence that is all that will be remembered of jazz.

POSTLUDE AND VALE

POSTLUDE

LOUIS CHESLOCK
(The Saturday Night Club)

FROM THE earliest days of his association with the *Herald*, Mencken sought out his colleagues on the staff who were in any way music-minded. If they could play or sing they met for musical evenings. Through Joseph Callahan, one of his associates, he met a number of better amateurs. Two of them joined forces with him and Callahan around 1902, and by 1904 the four were meeting regularly on Saturday nights. Mencken was the pianist, Callahan the feeble second fiddle, and Samuel Hamburger—then a pants salesman and later an electrician—the zealous first. The fourth member was Albert Hildebrandt, maker of and dealer in violins, and an ardent amateur 'cellist. These men formed the nucleus of the Saturday Night Club.

During the next several years more men were admitted to the group. Some of the performers were downright poor and some were highly skilled professionals. To be a member one had to be, first of all, a genuine lover of music. If he could play—fine! If not, he had to listen. His conversation had to be worth while, and he had to be able to hold his own at the beer table. Acceptance into the group had to be unanimous.

Perhaps brief biographies of some of them—the combination of whom seasoned and flavored the group—will help make better known the club's unusual character. Heinrich Ewald Buchholz was the financial editor of the *Herald*. His knowledge of music was limited, but he was excellent company. Later, when the club held its sessions in Hildebrandt's violin shop on Saratoga Street, instead of in the homes of members, and went afterward to the old Rennert Hotel, only a few steps away, Buchholz arranged the supper. But more important, he served as the club's librarian.

The first professional musician to join was Theodore Hemberger. Born in Bruchsal, Germany, in 1871, he came to Baltimore in 1903 after a ten-year stay in Pennsylvania, where he was the conductor of the Scranton Symphony Orchestra and of a large chorus, besides playing first violin in a string quartet. He was invited to Baltimore to accept the leadership of its well-known Germania Maennerchor. Shortly after his arrival he became director also of a number of other German singing societies and of Zion Lutheran Church. Later he became violin instructor at the Peabody Conservatory of Music. Mencken heard him play and he was elected to membership. His influence was immediately felt. He made arrangements of compositions to suit the limited number of players. It was "Theo H." who supplied Mencken with a piano version of the Brahms Second Symphony, played it over with him a number of times, and won him away from the biased view of Brahms he got from Wilberfoss G. Owst, the *Herald's* music critic.

Dr. John Wade had been a professional flute player when a young man. He played in the Monumental theatre, where some of Baltimore's most peppery burlesque shows were given. The salary helped pay his way through medical college. He was the first woodwind player to join the club. Another performing member who joined about 1910 was the famous anatomical artist, Max Brödel. Born in Leipzig in 1870, he was forced to begin the study of piano at the age of six by his music-loving father, Louis. His endless enthusiasm for playing the piano was no less than Mencken's, who played *secundo* to his *primo*.

A picture of the club taken in November, 1913, shows the following seated around the beer table in a private room reserved for them at the Rennert Hotel: Henry L. Mencken,* Samuel Hamburger,* Max Cathcart* (he played the piano, after a fashion, and was a good bass singer who knew every note of the Gilbert and Sullivan operettas), Paul Patterson (business manager of the Sunpapers), Frederick Colston,* Theodore Hemberger,* Harry Bush, Willard Huntington Wright (author of the famous Philo Vance mystery stories, published over the pseudonymn "S. S. Van Dyne"), Frederick A. Kummer, (author and playwright), Adelin Fermin (teacher of voice at the Peabody Conservatory, occasionally guest pianist with the club), Dr. John Wade,* Col. Joseph Wickes (employed at the Baltimore City Hall—he sometimes played the 'cello), Albert Hildebrandt,* John Phelps, Max Brödel,* Philip

Green (president of a local millwork plant), Matthew Tinker * (in charge of a local railroad terminal), Folger McKinsey * (the "Benztown Bard,"—poet for the Baltimore *Morning Sun*), David Bacharach * (eminent photographer), and Alexander H. McDannald.

Those with asterisks after their names were members. Absent at the time the picture was taken were Buchholz, Callahan and Prof. Blanckennagel (the latter a member of Goucher College faculty, who played flute and piccolo). Frequent guests at that time were: Carl Schon (maker of fine jewelry), Philip Goodman (publisher and theatrical producer), Ernest Boyd (British consul in Baltimore), Dr. Henry Flood, and Dr. John Ruhrah.

One of Mencken's oldest friends was native Baltimorean W. Edwin Moffett, who in his youth was a cornet player in a Sunday School group. Later he transferred from cornet to trombone, and played with the Peabody Symphony Orchestra. He gave up the trombone, too, to apply himself seriously to the study of the double bass. He became extremely proficient on the instrument and was made principal bass in the Baltimore Symphony Orchestra when it was founded in 1916.

Another distinguished professional musician was Dr. Gustav Strube. Born in Balenstedt, Germany, in 1867, he came to America in 1889 to be a violinist in the Boston Symphony Orchestra under Arthur Nikisch. Later he was made assistant conductor, and for ten years prior to leaving the orchestra he was also director of its "Pop" concerts. In 1913 he came to Baltimore to teach at the Peabody, and a

few years later was the organizer and conductor of the Baltimore Symphony Orchestra. He became a member of the
club in 1914. Some of his most charming, lighter works
were composed for the club.

Joining at this time also was the affable Adolph Torovsky.
A Bohemian by birth, he came to America while yet a
young man. He was not here long before he became the
bandmaster at the Naval Academy, where he remained until he retired in 1922. He then took charge of the music at
St. John's College in Annapolis. Torovsky was a musical
"natural," for he was able to perform well on nearly any
musical instrument. He preferred the strings, and these he
played most often. He was one of the club's best-loved
composers, writing for it the kind of music he remembered
from his youth—the lovely, nostalgic melodies of Bohemia
and Vienna.

William W. Woollcott, brother of the famous Alexander, became a non-performing member around 1917. His
home in Catonsville, a suburb of Baltimore, was the site, in
1922, of a brave attempt by the club to play, then and there
and one after another, the first eight of Beethoven's symphonies. The idea was Woollcott's. The attempt, of course,
came to grief, but a lot of fun was had. Willie wrote the
words and music of the club's own anthem, "I am a 100%
American." Mencken picked out the notes for him on the
piano and Hemberger harmonized it. The piece found its
way into print and is now widely known.

Dr. Franklin Hazlehurst was one of Mencken's boyhood
friends. The family lived on Hollins Street near the Menck-

ens. Upon his graduation from Hopkins, Frank went to Germany for further study. He became an eye-ear-nose-and-throat specialist. He played the violin and 'cello.

Raymond Pearl, Professor of Biology at Johns Hopkins, played the French horn.

Old Dr. Christian Deetjen, of German stock but born in Brazil, became a member in the early 1920's. When a young man he had been sent to Germany for his medical education. He was among the pioneers in radiology, and because the risks in this work were not sufficiently known at the time, his hands became badly burned and disfigured. His hobbies were folk medicine, witchcraft and the distillation of fine liqueurs. He was a non-playing member. Dr. Max Kahn, another radiologist, was one too.

Israel Dorman's talent for violin was recognized when he was a student at the Peabody, and on graduation he was appointed a teacher in its Preparatory Department. For a long time, also, he played first violin in the Baltimore Symphony. He joined the club sometime in the mid-1920's.

For many years these were the chief members of the club, and they remained members to the end of their days, or until the club disbanded. I first heard Henry Mencken play the piano more than thirty years ago at the home of Gustav Strube. The program opened with the Cesar Franck symphony. From the first notes it was obvious that Mencken knew his music. With each new shift in tempo and tonality he was the soul of the ensemble. Sudden *pianissimo*—and he hushed the bass and horn. He signaled each entry. And so it went through exposition, development, recapitulation and into the coda. And at the end he let out an enormous whoop.

When Dr. Wade died, around 1931, the club had great difficulty in finding another agreeable flutist. But a couple of years later Buchholz introduced Frank Purdum, a prosperous druggist, who played the flute with us several times as a guest before he was made a member. Shortly after, Mencken's brother, August (engineer and author), became a non-performing member.

With the passing of Albert Hildebrandt, in 1932, the club found itself even harder pressed for another 'cellist. We had a number of good guest players. but it was not until five years later that the club found in Samuel Dorman, Israel's younger brother, the man they wanted. But, unhappily, he, too, died shortly afterward, and the 'cello parts for a long time thereafter were played by Torovsky or Hazlehurst. During the next several years (1939–46) the club suffered a series of appalling losses: Pearl, Brödel, Deetjen, Torovsky, Hazlehurst, and Purdum.

Around 1942, Dr. Arnold R. Rich, Professor of Pathology at Johns Hopkins, joined us with his viola. (He and I have facetiously engaged in a running duel since we first met on the question of what does or does not constitute a folksong.) [1]

About two years later, George Newcomer, a lawyer, joined to play second violin. Then followed Robert Waite, a 'cellist. He came from Indiana, was in government employ,

[1] See Mencken's article, "The Music of the American Negro," (p. 153) which is the view, I too, have always held.

and introduced by Newcomer. In 1945, James M. Cain, who had been a frequent guest, became the only non-resident member, and thus allowed to pay his own check at supper. (It was a rule of the club that a guest could not pay for his food or treat the club or any of its members. Nor could any member treat the club except on his birthday, when he paid for a round of beers. Incidentally, the club never accepted invitations to meet away from home.) For a short time in 1948–9, Dr. Joseph Blum played the violin and viola.

After the death of Max Brödel, in 1941, Mencken asked me to take over *primo* piano, where I remained until the break-up of the club nine years later. Playing beside Mencken was an exhilarating experience.

The club's library contained approximately 500 works, including nearly all the standard symphonies, as well as many well-known overtures, tone-poems and suites. Most of the classical chamber music repertoire was there, too, and an amazing number of waltzes, marches, and selections from operas and operettas, as well as popular pieces like "Old Man River," and "The Beer Barrel Polka." Included were a number of rare works, some out of print. And, of course, the many original pieces written by members. While everyone chipped in from time to time to meet the cost of some music, most of the library was contributed by Mencken.

During Prohibition days the club met at the homes of members, but with Repeal we went back to Hildebrandt's shop (now located on St. Paul Street) and to the Rennert for supper. But the old hotel was no longer the charming place it had been, and after some trial meetings at other restaurants we found what we wanted in a private room at Schellhase's.

Throughout the near half-century of its existence the club met every Saturday night. Only if Christmas night might fall on a Saturday, and once, to attend the premiere of a ballet by one of its composer members, did the group omit its meeting.

Henry Mencken's outlet for music-making was almost exclusively in the Saturday Night Club. He rarely missed a meeting. When he suffered a stroke in 1948, and could no longer play, his interest in music did not wane. He sent word from the hospital that he hoped the club would continue and that he could return to it soon himself. During his long illness he listened nightly to radio broadcasts of good music. Throughout the winter months he tuned in on Saturdays to the Metropolitan broadcasts when they did Mozart, Strauss, or Wagner. Alfred Knopf sent him a good phonograph on his return home and he enjoyed listening to recordings of his favorite composers.

Toward the close of 1950 it became apparent that the club had seen its best days. On December 2, 1950, a meeting was held in which it was resolved that the weekly musical sessions be permanently discontinued, and the library be presented to the Enoch Pratt Free Library. The action was immediately carried out and this marked the end of the Saturday Night Club. A few of the members continued for a short time to meet sporadically on Saturday nights for beer and talk, but soon these meetings, too, came to an end.

VALE

LOUIS CHESLOCK

Until the time of his final illness it had been customary for Mencken, while still associated with the Sunpapers, to write an obituary on the passing away of a club member. The one given here, on Albert Hildebrandt, reveals a warm tenderness and deep feeling for his lifelong friend, who was, with him, one of the original members of the Saturday Night Club. I believe that its writing must have come to him in the form of music.[1] If it were translated into tone it might very well become a *Canto Elegia, con amore.*

The End of a Happy Life

From the Baltimore *Evening Sun*, November 21, 1932.

The late Albert Hildebrandt, who died last Thursday, had barely turned sixty, but he really belonged to an older Balti-

[1] "When I think of anything properly describable as a beautiful idea, it is always in the form of music." (*Happy Days*. New York: Alfred A. Knopf; 1940, p. 196.)

more, and it was far more charming than the Rotarian Gehenna we endure today. He was one of its genuine no-tables, though he got into the newspapers very seldom. What kept him out was mainly his own surpassing ami-ability: he was completely innocent of that yearning to harass the neighbors which commonly passes among us as public spirit. If he ever made a speech it must have been be-fore I met him, which was more than thirty years ago. When the Babbitts of the town held a banquet and afflicted one another sadly he stayed at home, playing the violoncello, or went to a beerhouse for a decent evening with his friends. When a public committee was appointed to improve man-kind and solve the insoluble he was not on it.

Nevertheless, there were few Baltimoreans of his time who were better worth knowing, for he stood in the first rank of a very difficult profession. He practiced it all his life with unfailing devotion and complete honesty, and that practice not only engrossed him but also pleasantly entertained him, and made him content. He enjoyed violins as other men enjoyed pictures or books. When he encountered a good one he would strip off his coat and have at it with the enthusiasm of a Schliemann unearthing a new Troy, and when a bad one came into his hands he would demolish its pretensions with a gusto but little less. If his judgement was ever questioned, it was not by sensible men. He was so obviously the master of his subject that, once he had ex-pressed his views and offered his reasons, there was no an-swer short of complaining to the police.

There were chances in his business for considerable killings, but he seldom took advantage of them. His attitude toward the violins that passed through his hands was commonly more sentimental than commercial, and he spent a lot of time and energy upon labors that brought him little profit, and sometimes not even thanks. It always seemed to me that a sort of professional delicacy stayed him—that he was too sensitive about the honor of his distinguished house, and had too much respect for violins themselves, to traffic in them too brutally. When the impulse to pile up money came upon him he always turned to some other enterprise, usually highly speculative. That other enterprise was never a shining success, but while it lasted it at least gave him the feeling that, within the bounds of his vocation, he could remain the free artist, and suffer no compulsion to approach the unseemly, which was to him the impossible.

His instrument, as I have said, was the 'cello, which he mastered in early youth, and stuck to faithfully all his life. Violins were always in his hands, but he never ventured to play them, and in fact had no talent for the business. But as a 'cellist he had great skill, and in the Baltimore of his day there was no amateur to match him. He was a big fellow, tall, muscular, handsome and imposing, and he had a tone to go with his size. When he would get a good grip upon his bow and fall upon a passage to his taste the sounds that came out of his 'cello were like an army with banners. Moreover, they were the precise sounds that stood in the score, for he had a fine ear and he played in tune all the way up the scale, even to the treacherous peaks of the A string.

He remained strictly an amateur to the end. He was often besought to play professionally, but he always refused. Years ago he was a member of the Haydn and Garland Orchestras and other such amateur organizations, and often appeared in public, sometimes as a soloist, but as he grew older he withdrew from this activity, and confined himself to playing with his family and his friends. So long as St. Mary's Seminary was in operation in Paca Street, he played there at the midnight mass every Christmas Eve. He was completely empty of piety, but he got on very well with the clergy, and one of his close friends was the late Dr. Theodore C. Foote, of St. David's, Roland Park, another amateur 'cellist. More than once I have done accompaniments to their duets, with each exhorting the other to lay on, and the evening ending with the whole band exhausted.

On the secular side he got through almost everything written for the 'cello. For twenty-five years he went to the late Frederick H. Gottlieb's house every Sunday night to engage in chamber music, and even longer he played every Saturday night with another club. Nor was this all, for he put in many evenings playing with his wife, his daughter and his sister-in-law, and in the earlier days there were weeks when he made music every night. He was always ready to drop everything for a session with his 'cello. Once, years ago, I happened into his place one afternoon when a German exchange student was calling on him. The German allowed that he was a fiddler, and Al suggested a couple of trios. We played from 4 to 6:30, went out to dinner, returned at 7:30, and kept on until 11. Another time he was a party to a desperate scheme to play the first eight Beethoven symphonies *seriatim*. We began late one afternoon, and figured that, allowing for three suppers, one breakfast, one lunch, and five pauses for wind and beer, the job would take 24 hours. But we blew up before we got to the end of the Eroica.

The headline that I have put on these lines indicates that this was a happy man. I believe that, in all my days, I have never known a happier. There were some people he disliked, and in discussing them he was capable of a blistering invective, but on the whole he was too good-humored to have enemies, and he got on well even with musicians, who are sometimes very difficult. He was a bachelor for many years, but he was always quartered with friends, and so had a comfortable home. He made a good living, spent his money freely, had a civilized taste for sound eating and drinking, and never tired of music for an instant. When he married, relatively late in life, his luck remained with him, and he was presently the center of a charming family circle, with a little daughter whose precocious talent gave him great delight. He had a long and trying illness, but he was nursed with singular devotion and his doctor was an old and valued friend—and, I hope I need not add a fiddler too. He faced death calmly, and slipped into oblivion at last with simple courage and no foolish regrets.

Such a man, it seems to me, comes very close to the Aristotelian ideal of the good citizen and the high-minded man. There was no pretension in him, but his merits were solid and enduring. He possessed a kind of knowledge that was not common, and it was very useful. He treated his clients with great scrupulosity, and his professional reputation, unchallenged for many years, went far beyond the bounds of Baltimore. He was so unfailingly kindly, so thoroughly square and decent, so completely lovable that the whole world that he knew was filled with his friends. Most of his leisure, in his later days, was spent with men he played with, musically and otherwise, for twenty, thirty and even forty years. The old-timers all stuck to him, and there were always youngsters coming in, to learn him and love him. Save when illness made a prisoner of him he saw them constantly, and even as he lay dying he knew that he was in their daily thoughts, and would never pass out of their memories.

They drop off one by one—Sam Hamburger, Phil Green, John Wade, Carl Schon, Henry Flood, Fred Colston, Charlie Bochau, and now Al Hildebrandt. These were pleasant fellows, one and all. The common bond between them was their love of music, and I suppose that there is no better to be found. Certainly there can be none that makes life more genuinely cheerful and contented. Most of the men I have named were amateurs, and some were only listeners, but they had in common that amiable weakness for the squeaks of the fiddle and the burble of the flute, and it kept them together for long years. They clustered around Al Hildebrandt. He was, in his way, the best friend of every one of them, and he remains the best friend of many who still live.

Mourning him would be rather silly. He died too soon,

but so do we all. The universe is run idiotically, and its only certain product is sorrow. But there are yet men who, by their generally pleasant spirits, by their intense and enlightened interest in what they have to do, by their simple dignity and decency, by their extraordinary capacity for making and keeping friends, yet manage to cheat, in some measure, the common destiny of mankind, doomed like the beasts to perish. Such a man was Albert Hildebrandt. It was a great privilege to be among his intimates; he radiated a sound and stimulating philosophy, and it was contagious. In all my days I have known no other who might have taken to himself with more reason the words of the ancient poet: "The lines are fallen unto me in pleasant places; yea, I have a goodly heritage."

INDEX OF COMPOSERS

AND PERFORMERS

H. L. MENCKEN

was born in Baltimore in 1880 and died there in 1956. Educated privately and at Baltimore Polytechnic, he began his long career as journalist, critic, and philologist on the Baltimore *Morning Herald* in 1899. In 1906 he joined the staff of the Baltimore *Sun*, thus initiating an association with the *Sun* papers which lasted until a few years before his death. He was co-editor of the *Smart Set* with George Jean Nathan from 1908 to 1923, and with Nathan he founded in 1924 the *American Mercury*, of which he was editor until 1933. His numerous books include *A Book of Burlesques* (1916); *A Book of Prefaces* (1917); *In Defense of Women* (1917); *The American Language* (1918—4th revision, 1936); *Supplement One* (1945); *Supplement Two* (1948); six volumes of *Prejudices* (1919, 1920, 1922, 1924, 1926, 1927); *Notes on Democracy* (1926); *Treatise on the Gods* (1930); *Treatise on Right and Wrong* (1934); *Happy Days* (1940); *Newspaper Days* (1941); *Heathen Days* (1943); *A Mencken Chrestomathy* (1949); and *Minority Report* (1956). Mencken also edited several books; he selected and edited *A New Dictionary of Quotations* (1942). He was co-author of a number of books, including *Europe after 8:15* (1914); *The American Credo* (1920); *Heliogabalus* (a play, 1920); and *The Sunpapers of Baltimore* (1937).

A NOTE ON THE TYPE

THIS BOOK is set in Electra, a Linotype face designed by the late W. A. Dwiggins (1880–1956). This face cannot be classified as either modern or old style. It is not based on any historical model, nor does it echo any particular period or style. It avoids the extreme contrasts between thick and thin elements that mark most modern faces, and attempts to give a feeling of fluidity, power, and speed.

Composed, printed, and bound by
Kingsport Press, Inc., Kingsport, Tenn.
Paper manufactured by
S. D. Warren Co., Boston.
Typography and binding design
based on originals by
W. A. DWIGGINS